P9-BIH-723

RECCHIETTE. GNOCCHI RICCI.
AFFRON AND POTATO GNOCCHI
ICOTTA GNOCHETTI. CAZZELLIT
OYALE BOLOGNESE. DONDERET
NOCCHI ALLA BAVA. FRASCARE
UGELI. CHICKPEA GNOCCHETTI
UCKWHEAT AND RICOTTA GNOC
NOCCHI ALL' ORTICA. DUNDER:
ISAREI E FASO. RICOTTA CAVAT
EMOLINA TROFIE. PASSATELLI.
TROZZAPRETI. RUSTIC MALFAT
HICCHE DELLA NONNA. PINCI.
ICIONES. CECAMARITI. DONZEL
ASTA GRATTUGIATA. SORCETTI

PASTA BY HAND

PASTA
BY
HAND

A COLLECTION OF ITALY'S
REGIONAL HAND-SHAPED PASTA

JENN LOUIS

Foreword by **Mario Batali**

Photographs by Ed Anderson

CHRONICLE BOOKS
SAN FRANCISCO

Copyright © 2015 by Jenn Louis.

All rights reserved. No part of this book may be reproduced in any form without written permission from the publisher.

Library of Congress Cataloging-in-Publication Data available.

ISBN 978-1-4521-2188-8

Manufactured in China

Designed by Alice Chau

Photographs by Ed Anderson
Food styling by George Dolese
The photographer wishes to thank Jenn Louis and David Welch for their hospitality, generosity, and great on-set breakfasts; George Dolese for his light-handed sense of style that makes every shot sing; and the friendly city of Portland, Oregon.

10 9 8 7 6 5

Chronicle Books LLC
680 Second Street
San Francisco, California 94107
www.chroniclebooks.com

To everyone who cares about everything and who knows that the little things are what matter most.

ACKNOWLEDGMENTS

Thank you to all of the Italians and Italian Americans who generously shared their culture with me.

Thank you to everyone who has believed in me, supported me, and been patient with me.

Andrew Sessa, Kathleen Squires, Ed Anderson, and George Dolese, thank you for taking a great interest in a project so important to me.

Zaffy and Denis, thank you for sharing so much love with me and teaching me the importance of community.

Thank you to my pop, Jeff. I am so grateful for our relationship. I love you. And thank you to my brother, David, and my sister, Stacy.

Thank you to my wonderfully lovely husband, David. Thank you for always being at my side. I love you more than anything.

In loving memory of my mother, Isabel. I will bake your challah recipe as many Fridays as I can.

I have this joke about Italians: When you have ten Italians in a room, you have fourteen opinions.

CONTENTS

SAUCES 170

LARDER 188

FOREWORD

The chef world is growing more and more crowded every day. On just about every cable and network TV channel, there are chef competition shows featuring lesser-known chefs vying for fame, fortune, and their own 15 minutes, who are judged by other chefs who have moved up the reality-program ranks and are venerated, at least for the moment, as king and queen chefs. There are iron chefs, top chefs, kid chefs, master chefs, biker chefs, rock-and-roll chefs, late-night chefs, and daytime network chefs. In the summer of 2014, there were three full-length feature films in national release about chefs with the word "chef" in the title. Chefs are media hot.

It seems to me that these TV/media chefs are so busy that there is very little time between the hours spent in the makeup room, in media training, with stage hands, with prop stylists, and with camera crews to actually cook. What is becoming rarer is the chef who spends time researching and devising true and self-fulfilling deliciousness. Balancing the very important role of promotion and the even more important role of creating tasty and thoughtful food on a daily basis is tough business. When I scan a city for a visit, I am most happy when I find a chef who values his or her own craft over making morning show appearances. That is not to say that I do not love dining at restaurants run by chefs who have serious media presence, such as Emeril Lagasse, Bobby Flay, Michael Symon, and Wolfgang Puck. But every now and then I find or meet a chef who is so thoughtful and passionate about cooking that I'm inspired to get to the market, feel renewed excitement at the stove, and am reminded about the true joy of food.

Jenn Louis is such a chef.

Jenn's enthusiasm about food, cooking, and life is exciting. It is written into every email or text message she has ever sent me. It is epidemic. And her passion is both thrilling and disruptive. In her relentless search for the authentic, the real, the traditional, and the not-so-obvious, she has traveled to nearly all of the magnificent and unique regions in the boot of Italy looking for the comprehensive truth and all-encompassing enlightenment about . . . dumplings? Oh yes she has.

One of the main objectives of the Slow Food movement is to define and maintain rich regional traditions, ingredients, techniques, and products as a defense against the commercialization and homogenization and the subsequent or eventual loss of these cornerstones of excellence. The handmade Italian dumpling is indeed an exquisite example of a food well worth our "Slow" attention. Eschewing dried pasta, stuffed pasta, baked pasta, pasta asciutta, and all other forms of the glorious category called *primi* in Italian, Jenn has spent countless hours of research and travel pursuing the humble and magnificent category of dumpling, what Italians call *gnocchi*. And we the readers can say *beati noi*, which loosely translates from Italian to "lucky (or more precisely, blessed) us."

Jenn has uncovered and brought to light such delicious (I only surmise) and traditional dishes as frascarelli, dunderi, and ciciones. As intuitive as these dumplings seem to me now that I see them on Jenn's pages, their existence and the fact that I have never tasted them, let alone heard of them, cause me to question the depth of my own commitment to Italian regional cooking. But I am not dismayed. No, I am excited. My work is rejuvenated by the new, for me, wrinkle in the complex and infinite delights of Italian gastronomy.

In all of my years traveling similar roads doing similar-minded research to Jenn's, I have never encountered such a magnificent single-topic cookbook as *Pasta by Hand*. This spectacular volume is poetically inspirational and defines the work of "the chef" in the twenty-first century well beyond the world of broadcast and Internet programming. But for me, *Pasta by Hand* will be a marker, a moment in time, from which I will forever measure a renewal of my passion as a chef. It has given new breath to my life's project and my search for delicious and authentic foods that are expressions of joy and love in a pot or on a plate. And for that I thank you, Chef Louis.

MARIO BATALI

TRENTINO-
ALTO ADIGE

FRIULI-VENEZIA GIULIA

VALLE
D'AOSTA

LOMBARDY

VENETO

PIEDMONT

EMILIA-ROMAGNA

LIGURIA

TUSCANY

MARCHE

UMBRIA

ABRUZZO

LAZIO

MOLISE

PUGLIA

CAMPANIA

BASILICATA

SARDINIA

CALABRIA

SICILY

INTRODUCTION

I was backpacking in Europe when I first ate authentic Italian gnocchi. It was twenty years ago, and I had just graduated from college. Throughout the trip, I mostly ate bread, cheese, or whatever I could afford, keeping a few staples in my daypack to sustain myself. It was not extravagant fare. One dark December evening, I found myself in a restaurant in Siena, Tuscany. It was an ancient structure, tucked into a catacomb of winding cobblestone walkways. It was 6 P.M., and though I was the only one dining that early, the restaurant was open and I was hungry. I splurged on potato gnocchi with basil pesto, and I was in love after just one bite.

When we were preparing to open Lincoln Restaurant in 2008, I considered using dried pasta, but after we opened serving fresh, handmade pasta, I knew we could never do anything less. I wanted our guests to have a special experience eating fresh pasta, as I had with those first gnocchi in Siena. Fresh pasta was a part of our commitment to our customers: everything we serve would be made by hand. We would always carefully consider which pastas we would make and which sauces we would pair with them. We started with cavatelli (ricotta and semolina), pappardelle, and fettuccine, and then we began to research more interesting regional pastas. We made lasagnette (with white wine), malloreddus (with saffron from Sardinia), and tajarin (angel-hair pasta from Piedmont). We varied the offering based on the season.

As I learned more about the different classes of pasta, I became inspired by Italian dumplings. Like most Americans, the only Italian dumplings I had known of were tender potato gnocchi. But once I started to make different varieties of dumplings at Lincoln, such as sorcetti and malloreddus, they became a standard on the menu. I couldn't stop researching the subject, and I made it a rule that we always would offer at least one variety of gnocchi. (The subject of what a dumpling is is somewhat complicated. I'll explain later; read on.)

After collecting about twenty-five recipes, I decided to put together a book, but every time I researched a region or a specific dumpling, I found more and more examples of historic and delicious Italian dumplings. There is no authoritative collection of dumpling recipes written in English, and—much to my surprise—I was not able to find one in Italian. Often, pasta books and Italian cookbooks will include a few dumpling recipes, but I never found a single comprehensive source. And because many traditional recipes are passed along orally rather than written down, I began to collect and catalog as many as I could.

At this point, "gnocchi" escalated from a point of curiosity to a genuine research project. As part of my research, I talked to as many people as I possibly could: fellow cooks from around the world, food scholars, my customers, Italians, Italian Americans. Did they make it (or at least eat it) when they were growing up? What were the ingredients? How was it prepared? Did they call it *gnocchi*, or did it have another name? I used these casual interviews—they were brief oral histories, essentially—to complement what I had previously found. For every variation on dumplings, every anecdote, I dug deeper to see what else I could find.

What I found was that this book was not going to be easy. At every turn, I found another unique dumpling with a story behind it. On one hand, I had more information about Italian dumplings than I could ever have hoped for. On the other hand, I had more questions than answers.

So after I did all of the research I could in the United States, I went to Italy with my husband, David. We rented a Fiat (naturally) and drove around the country. The trip was amazing; it was one of the most exciting experiences of my career and was critical to writing this book.

———

Italy was not formally unified as a country until 1861, which makes it almost one hundred years younger than the United States. At the same time, the regional cultures and traditions within Italy are ancient, firmly rooted, and very proud. The result, at least as it relates to something as meaningful and visceral as food, is a vast difference of opinion that is deeply held and fiercely defended from region to region.

As we traveled through Italy, each person I interviewed and cooked with had a different notion about what was and was not gnocchi. When I approached the subject as *dumplings*, I was quickly corrected and told that dumplings are Chinese food. (This was accompanied by a smirk and shake of the head in many cases.) And while there is no word for *dumpling* in Italian, the singular form of gnocchi—*gnocco*—translates into English as "dumpling." There were no clear rules for defining dumplings as a category. Some considered gnocchi to be strictly small handmade potato dumplings. When I loosely defined "dumpling" to them, they conceded that some handmade pasta shapes, with or without potato, would fall into the "dumpling" category. Some dumplings were tender and light, others were more toothy and dense, due to their specific ingredients. Although many regions share very similar names for their dumplings, the recipes can contain very different ingredients.

So here I was with so many great recipes and so much rich information about these rustic, comforting little bits of dough. And while my Italian friends may not agree (OK, they absolutely will not agree), I needed to come to some kind of unifying definition.

So here is my working definition of Italian dumplings: carefully handcrafted nubs of dough that are poached, simmered, baked, or sautéed. The category is large, as these dumplings vary in shape, size, and texture. I decided to leave pasta ripiena (stuffed pastas like ravioli and agnolotti) out of this, since they already belong to another clearly defined category. Some dumplings have the word *gnocchi* in their name and some don't, depending on the traditions of a specific village or region. And while all gnocchi are dumplings, not all dumplings are gnocchi. Italian dumplings can be made from a variety of ingredients—potato, cheese, greens, or grains. They can be cooked by a variety of methods—simmering, braising, or sautéing. This in turn gives them a wide range of textures. They can be dense and chewy, with a satisfyingly firm bite. Or they can be soft, light, and almost airy. Some are made from potato and rolled into small handmade pieces; others are made from spoonfuls of ricotta gently dropped into simmering water, yielding a soft, tender, irregularly shaped dumpling. Some have specific names (sorcetti, malfatti, gnudi) while others are called gnocchi, gnocchi verdi (green gnocchi), or chicche (the northern Italian dialect for the word *gnocchi*). Some recipes in this book bridge the gap between traditional Italian categories of pastina (small pasta), pasta corta (short pasta), and gnocchi that are served with sauce or used in soups.

While they have not been clearly or consistently defined throughout Italy, dumplings have a very important and beloved place in the world of Italian cooking. Regional disagreements aside, the dumplings in this book are here because they fit my working definition, and they are undeniably satisfying. All recipes are handmade, not rolled and cut or extruded through a machine. There will always be room for debate, but there is one matter on which we can agree: Whatever we choose to call them, Italian dumplings are rustic, toothsome, comforting, and some of the most soulful Italian food we can eat.

————

Our time in Italy was inspiring. It was delicious, and it was life changing. I will never forget the lessons I learned from my mentors and the generosity with which they shared their expertise. Fun as it was, the trip was intense and hard work. Our days were dictated by a strict routine. We woke up every morning, packed our luggage into the car, and drove anywhere between thirty minutes and two hours to a new lesson from a restaurant chef or home cook. After every lesson, we drove on to the next town or city,

up to five hours away. While David drove, I set up a makeshift office in the front seat and immediately read over my notes. I typed the recipes and methods I learned while they were still fresh in my mind. At the end of the day, we checked in to a new hotel. We slept in a new bed almost every night for sixteen nights. Then the next morning the routine would start again.

My mentors were truly wonderful. They ranged in age from thirty-five to seventy and lived in a variety of delightful communities. Some of my mentors lived on rural winery estates, while others lived in central Rome. We even traveled to the northern mountainous region of the Dolomites.

Regardless of the mentor or the location, I had a nearly identical experience every time I started a lesson: I was viewed with skepticism until I got my hands on the dough and started to tell my mentor about my book. As soon as they saw my comfort in the kitchen and my experience making dumplings, I was part of the club. We talked about flour types, kneading, their memories of eating dumplings as children, and how the neighboring village's dumplings were nowhere near as wonderful as the dumplings of their village. Every day, I built strong and special relationships with those who taught me. It was an amazing experience. My mentors taught me with openness and pride. At the end of every lesson, we would sit at a table and eat together. We drank wine, of course, ate what we had made, and gained admiration for each other. We shared a sense of craftsmanship, tradition, and the meaning and value of hospitality.

All my mentors wondered why a Jewish girl from Portland, Oregon, wanted to learn about their dumplings. When I shared with them my sincere caring and enthusiasm for the subject, they opened their world even more, offering to teach me additional dishes and methods that went beyond our original plan. And because of this, my Italian dumpling recipe collection continued to grow!

I was taught an ancient tradition that was soulful and delicious, but I began to realize that the tradition was being lost. Handmade dumplings take time and skill to make, and the craft of dumpling making is practiced less and less in Italian homes. This tradition is a national treasure, and not only has it never before been documented in a collection, but it is in danger of being forgotten.

When I returned home, I tested every recipe with the ingredients that were available to me. American flour is different from Italian flour, as are the potatoes, ricotta, and many other ingredients. I learned the importance of using a digital scale to weigh ingredients by grams. Although Italian dumplings are rustic, making the very best dumplings is a craft that requires strict attention to detail. Consistently good results are achieved with careful measuring of ingredients until you have a good feel for a dough's ideal texture and consistency.

The dumplings in this book are faithful documentations of what I learned from Italian and American chefs, nonnas, and home cooks. All recipe quantities are representations of the amounts that I learned when first making them. Some produce larger quantities than others, but all of them can be multiplied in size or reduced as needed. These recipes are regional and therefore based on local, traditional methods, using ingredients that were close at hand.

I know that I will continue to learn to make dozens more Italian dumplings—the Italian tradition is deep, and many small villages and individual families continue to practice their unique variations. This book just happens to be my collection. I really love making, serving, and eating these dumplings, at Lincoln and in my home. I hope you love them, too.

THE BASICS

While gnocchi reward patience and attention to detail, most are not very hard to make. The pages that follow outline the specific ingredients, tools, and techniques that will help you craft rustic, savory, and satisfying dumplings.

BREAD CRUMBS, CHEESE, EGGS, FLOUR, GREENS, AND POTATOES

The following ingredients are the essentials for making Italian dumplings. The most important thing to keep in mind while sourcing them is quality. Best-quality ingredients always ensure the most delicious results.

BREAD CRUMBS

Fresh bread crumbs are simply that: crumbs of bread. They are also made simply, by chopping soft bread, by hand or in a food processor, to the desired size and texture.

Dried bread crumbs (*pangrattato*) are made by removing the crust and cubing the loaf into 2-in (5-cm) cubes, then baking them in a 350°F (180°C) oven until they're completely dry. After they have cooled, pulse them in a food processor to make very fine crumbs.

Traditionally, **stale bread** (*raffermo*) is used in dumplings such as canederli. It is cubed and left overnight to dry, uncovered, on a baking sheet. Different types of bread will yield different results, so determining the type of bread needed for the specific dumpling is important. Some Italian villages produce only one type of bread, so naturally the gnocchi of that region is made using that bread.

CHEESE

Many types of cheese are used in making gnocchi. Traditionally, each dumpling will feature a cheese from its local region, but in recent years, cooks are willing to alter dishes by substituting another cheese, according to their own preference.

Parmigiano-Reggiano is a hard grating cheese made from raw cow's milk that is often called the "King of Cheeses." The name *Parmigiano-Reggiano* in Italy is a protected designation of origin, or DOP (Denominazione d'Origine Protetta), which means that similar cheeses made outside of the specified area may not use the name *Parmigiano-Reggiano*.

Grana is a hard cheese made from cow's milk. It is less sharp in flavor than Parmigiano-Reggiano and has less graininess and a less crystalline texture. It is suitable for grating. Several styles are made throughout Italy, such as grana Trentino and grana Padano.

Pecorino-Romano is a hard sheep's milk cheese that's originally from Rome, though most Pecorino-Romano is now made in Sardinia. Pecorino-Romano is best known for its sharp, salty quality; it is a favorite for pairing with pasta sauces.

The fresh cheese **ricotta** can be made from cow's, buffalo's, goat's, or sheep's milk. All types of ricotta will work for the recipes in this book. Look for fresh ricotta that has enough moisture to make it spreadable, but be sure the cheese is not sitting in any liquid. If your ricotta has liquid pooling, drain it with cheesecloth or a fine-mesh sieve to remove excess moisture. It is a simple and very satisfying process to make your own ricotta at home; see page 190 for my recipe.

EGGS

Always use the highest-quality chicken eggs you can find. Cage-free chickens that are fed a vegetarian diet will give your gnocchi the richness and texture you are looking for. These recipes all presume the use of U.S. large eggs, U.K. medium eggs.

FLOUR

Always store flour in an airtight container. At room temperature, it will keep for up to 4 months. If you do not use flour on a regular basis, store it in an airtight container or resealable bag in the freezer for up to 6 months. If flour is stored for too long, it becomes too dry and will absorb moisture differently from fresh flour.

The grains of different wheat varieties, and the flours made from them, range from soft to very hard. The hard varieties of wheat are higher in gluten. **Durum flour** is finely ground from durum wheat, which is the hardest variety of wheat. It is slightly yellow in color and sometimes called golden durum flour. It is high in protein and creates strong dough.

Gluten-free flour is a combination of flours from a variety of grains and starches that do not contain gluten, such as rice, corn, taro, and soy. I have tested a few of them, and each time the gluten-free flour yielded tender gnocchi. If you prefer this kind of flour for your dumplings, it is a worthy substitute.

"00" flour, or "zero doppio" (double zero), is highly refined flour in which the bran and germ have been removed and the kernel is ground to the texture of talcum powder. American-made "00" flour is very high in protein and builds excellent gluten strands, making it a good choice for preparing breads or pasta dough but not most gnocchi. In Italy, most flour is ground to "00" but the gluten content varies, and each variation has a specific use, whether for pasta, bread, pastry, or otherwise. Any gnocchi in this book that specifies "00" flour is intended to be made with American "00" flour or Italian "00" flour for pasta, but you may substitute American all-purpose flour.

American **all-purpose flour** is not as fine as Italian "00" flour, but has similar gluten qualities. Made from a combination of hard and soft wheat, unbleached all-purpose flour offers a balance of strength and tenderness. As the name suggests, it is good for most baking and cooking projects, including dumplings. In Italy, the equivalent is called *farina bianca*, simply meaning "white flour."

Semolina flour is made from the coarse wheat middlings of durum wheat and is high in gluten. It absorbs moisture at a slower rate than all-purpose flour and is used in some dumplings. Due to its coarse texture, it works well for dusting the baking sheets that hold formed dumplings.

GREENS

There are many greens that can be used when making gnocchi. Italians typically use whichever greens are available, depending on the season.

Beet greens are the leafy greens that sprout aboveground when beets are grown. The greens are very dark in color and have veins running through them that match the color of the beet (red, yellow, or white). Discard the stem that connects the root to the leaf and cook the greens like any other leafy braising green. Beet greens have a vegetal flavor and are rich in iron and chlorophyll.

Bietole is the Italian word for **chard**, a leafy green used widely in many Mediterranean dishes. The stem color will vary depending on the variety of chard, and the vegetable is most often served either simply braised, or braised and stuffed. Discard the tougher ribs and cook the leaves, though the ribs are wonderful when pickled, so it is a good idea to save them for another project. Chard has a bright green, earthy, and lemony flavor.

Collard greens are rarely seen in Italy but are widely available throughout the United States. Related to cabbage and broccoli, collard greens are rich in iron and have a deep, vegetal flavor. Collards can be used if kale is unavailable.

There are many varieties of **kale** to choose from. I prefer lacinato kale, also called Tuscan kale or black kale, but any variety will work just fine when making dumplings. Discard the fibrous ribs before cooking and give a bit more time when blanching, as the structure of the leaves is a bit tougher than most tender greens and needs additional cooking time to reach tenderness. Flavors of kale varieties range from moderately earthy to intensely iron-rich and vegetal.

Mustard greens have the pungent flavor of mustard, cabbage, and horseradish. Widely used in Italian cuisine, smaller mustard leaves may be eaten raw but are typically cooked and served as a side dish or added to braises, stews, or soups. True to their name, mustard greens can range on the scale of slightly spicy to very spicy and taste of the bright, sharp flavor of mustard.

Spinach is widely available in many countries and very simple to cook. Discard any stems and blanch briefly. Spinach is very tender and only needs to be cooked for a minute or two. It is delicate, earthy, and sweet.

Turnip and **radish greens** are often overlooked and discarded when turnips and radishes are cooked. This is too bad, because they are wonderful, tender, and pack a tremendous amount of pungent and spicy flavor. They are best used in sauces and as accents in dumplings rather than as a main ingredient, because the intensity of their flavor can be overpowering.

BASIC GREENS PREPARATION

Remove any tough ribs from greens and blanch in a pot of generously salted boiling water. Greens that are more fibrous, such as lacinato kale, will take a few extra minutes to blanch, while tender greens like spinach and mustard greens will take just a minute. When tender, immediately plunge greens into ice water to stop cooking. When cool, remove the greens and wring out in a cloth until almost all the moisture has been strained out.

Remove any colored ribs before making the gnocchi to eliminate any discoloration of the dough. The challenge with red beet greens and greens with colored veins and ribs is that the color leaches out when cooked. If using greens with colored ribs to make dumplings, wring cooked leaves in a clean kitchen towel to dispel most of the red liquid, which can discolor the dumplings. No matter what the color, always wring out the leaves very well, because greens tend to hold water once blanched, and excess moisture will create dense, heavy, and unappealing dumplings.

POTATOES

Starchy, floury varieties of potatoes such as **Russet** or **Yukon gold** work best for dumplings. They are generally uniform in size and texture. Don't substitute lower-starch waxy potatoes such as red potatoes, fingerlings, creamers, and new potatoes, as they will yield gnocchi with a gummy texture.

Always use very warm, freshly boiled potatoes. When cooking potatoes, don't test them for doneness too many times with a skewer, as more holes in the potato will translate to more water absorbed into the potato. Higher water content in the potato will make a dumpling that is too dense and chewy.

Peel the potatoes, rice them, and make the dough as soon as they are cool enough to handle. Use a ricer or food mill for a fine-textured dumpling. Do not use a food processor, because it will make the potato texture gummy.

WEIGH INGREDIENTS FOR BEST RESULTS

Dumplings are rustic and simple and do not need to be perfect. However, measuring ingredients by weight will keep your dumplings consistent and successful. I recommend using a good digital scale. There is great difference between measuring by volume and by weight, and even measuring by ounces can cause more variance than measuring by grams, which is why the recipes in this book use gram weight as the primary measurement. There are many simple and inexpensive digital scales available. If you love to cook, invest in a good scale that can measure in grams.

BOWLS, PADDLES, SCOOPS, SPOONS, AND OTHER TOOLS

Some of the items in this section may be very familiar to you, and others may seem unfamiliar and specialized, but all of them are common in an Italian kitchen. They are essential equipment for making dumplings.

I use a **plastic curved bench scraper** or a heat-resistant silicone spatula for removing gnocchi dough from bowls. Leaving bits in your bowl could waste a whole dumpling or two!

I prefer a **straight-edge metal bench scraper** for cutting portions of dough to roll one at a time, or for cutting dumplings. This tool is also useful for transporting delicate or soft dumplings from the baking sheet to the cooking water. It is especially helpful with recipes such as Potato and Sculpit Gnocchi (page 140).

A variety of sizes of **nonreactive bowls** are helpful for mixing, resting, and holding dough without imparting off flavors. I prefer to use glass or stainless-steel bowls.

A **food mill** will help purée your potatoes to a smooth, uniform consistency. Make sure to cook your potatoes well, leaving no hard or uncooked lumps.

A **potato ricer** does the same job as a food mill—it just does it better. The potato ricer is a smaller tool and you'll need to make a few more batches to complete the work, but it will yield a lighter and finer texture.

A **gnocchi paddle** is used to form the traditional indentations you find in each gnocco, which hold sauce and contribute to their texture. I bought mine in Rome; actually, I bought two. You can buy yours from a range of online or in-store sources; they are very inexpensive. These are flat boards with a handle and a ridged shaping

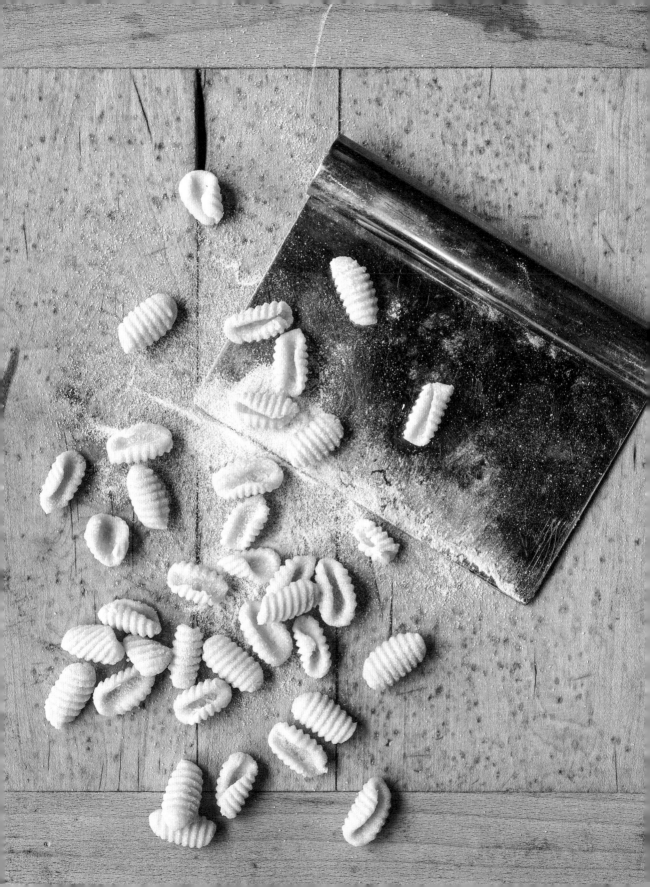

surface. You can use the tines on the back of a fork if you do not have a gnocchi paddle, and some cooks in Italy use the back of a nutmeg grater or fine cheese grater. Use one of these tools, as it is essential to create ridges on your gnocchi.

The #40 and #70 are my favorite sizes of **ice-cream scoops** for scooping malfatti and other round gnocchi dough. The number for each size refers to the number of scoops that will fit into a 1-qt (1-L) container. I like using these for consistency; each dumpling will be the same size and will therefore cook at the same rate. And while these are not strictly necessary—the same thing can be achieved with a couple of spoons—they make the process much easier.

If a digital scale is not available, use a set of **measuring cups** for the most accurate measure of dry ingredients. The best way to measure flour is the "scoop and sweep" method: Stir your flour so that it is not compacted, and dip your measuring cup into the flour. With a knife, ruler, or other straight-edge, level off the flour. This will yield the most uniformity when measuring ingredients. Use a **digital scale** for even more precision and consistency.

The fine-tooth **Microplane grater** is spectacular for making sure your nutmeg is finely grated, your lemon zest does not have bitter white pith attached, your garlic is as fine as it can be, and your cheese is delicately grated over your dumplings.

A small **paring knife** is a great tool for cutting many types of gnocchi. This does not need to be an expensive or fancy knife.

Parchment paper is a wonderful tool in the kitchen. It has a onetime use and is compostable. Use sheets of parchment to line your pan when baking cookies or when you roast a chicken. The paper makes cleanup a cinch.

When making dumplings, I like to line a baking sheet with parchment paper, dust the parchment with semolina flour or all-purpose flour, and put the formed gnocchi on it to dry. After the gnocchi have set up a bit, pull up the paper corners to help the gnocchi gently roll around in the flour and become evenly coated. You can buy small boxes of parchment paper in a roll or in individual sheets at the grocery store and large boxes at a restaurant supply store.

I like to have two **large shallow pots**: one for cooking gnocchi in plenty of salted water and another to finish the dumplings in warmed sauce. A deeper pot is helpful when blanching greens. Heavy-bottomed stainless-steel pans are the best to work with and, when properly cared for, will last a long time.

I recommend buying a few 13-by-18-in (33-by-46-cm) **baking sheets**. Take good care of them and they will last a long, long time.

Dumplings require a lot of mixing, and a good **heavy-duty stand mixer** is almost imperative for how it eases the task. I have always been pleased by the mixers made by KitchenAid. A stand mixer is an excellent tool for mixing dough, as well as for grinding meat (if you have the grinder attachment) for ragù.

A **spätzli maker** is a simple tool that does a great job of creating the drippy shape of spätzli with little mess. Basically, it is a grater that forms the dough into its distinctive shape. It is the same tool used to make German spaetzle (or spätzle).

TIPS FOR MAKING GREAT GNOCCHI

1. Use a scale to measure ingredients! You will have excellent consistency if you use a scale. The recipes in this book list gram measurements first, followed by volume measurements. Each person measures ingredients a little differently in a measuring cup, which can cause widely varying results. Having a simple kitchen scale that measures in grams will make all the difference.

2. Measure carefully, but trust your senses. There are many variables when making gnocchi: some eggs are slightly larger than others; some days you need to add more flour than usual; some stoves run hotter than others. It's important to measure precisely, but it's equally important to recognize when the dough is too dry or sticky. Many recipes in this book call for additional flour or liquid, as needed, to account for some of these variables. So pay close attention to the description of how the finished dough should look and feel and be ready to make adjustments to achieve the proper consistency.

3. When combining dough ingredients, Italian cooks traditionally mound the flour on a work surface and form a well in the center to hold the wet ingredients before drawing the flour into them. This method works perfectly and certainly has stood the test of time. When mixing dough myself, I put the ingredients in a bowl and use my hands or the hook attachment of a stand mixer, so this approach essentially mimics the traditional well method. I have found the results to be just as good as the traditional method.

4. Pay special attention to the mixing and cooking directions for each recipe. The mixing method for each dumpling dough will be different, to achieve the correct texture. Not all dumplings are meant to be tender and light.

5. Test your dough. When making dumplings, take one or two and put them in the simmering water. If they fall apart, add a bit more flour. You want just enough flour to prevent the dumplings from falling apart while cooking, and no more.

6. Ideally, dumplings are best eaten the day they are made. If you want to store them, remove excess flour and cover with an additional piece of parchment paper, cover with plastic wrap, and refrigerate. Many types of dumplings can be frozen for up to 1 month. To do so, freeze them on a parchment-lined baking sheet and, once frozen, transfer to an airtight container, such as a resealable plastic bag. When cooking frozen dumplings, always cook them directly from the freezer.

7. When measuring portions of most types of uncooked dumplings, we use a very specialized portioning tool at Lincoln: a teacup! When we opened the restaurant, we started using a teacup, which is really just 1 cup (240 ml), because the coffee station is next to the pasta station and all the teacups are right there, easy and accessible. We use a heaping cup for dumplings that have a simple sauce or a scant cup for dumplings that have a rich meat sauce.

8. Cook your gnocchi in abundantly seasoned— in other words, salted—water at a gentle simmer. I like to think of the water as the

seasoning of the pasta dough. As the water is absorbed by the dumpling as it cooks, the salt brings out the flavor of the dumpling. The water should be seasoned, but not salty. Simmer, do not boil. You should have moving bubbles, not a rapid boil, which can break apart your dumplings.

9. Don't overcook. Aim for al dente—that is, tender but still firm to the bite. *Al dente* literally translates as "to the tooth." I like to say that dumplings should have some toothiness but not stick in your molars. Most ricotta and potato gnocchi should be removed from simmering water when they start to bob and rise to the top of the pot. If your dumplings cook for too long, they will absorb too much water and become dense and overly chewy. Some dumplings need to cook longer; gnocchi made from semolina and chestnut flour are denser and require more cooking time. In general, dumplings cook for no more than 2 or 3 minutes. Frozen dumplings will require another 1 or 2 minutes.

10. Use a slotted spoon to remove your poached dumplings from the water, and finish cooking them by gently simmering them in warm sauce for 1 minute. If your sauce is too thick, add 2 Tbsp of the pasta cooking water to it.

11. For most dumplings, the sauce is not merely a dressing for the dumplings. The addition of sauce is actually the final step in completing the dish, because the dumplings are cooked briefly in the pan with the prepared sauce. Almost all dumpling recipes in this book are followed by suggested sauce pairings. At the end of each sauce

recipe, you'll find detailed instructions for finishing the dumpling recipes.

12. Nothing is perfect. These are wonderful handmade dumplings, and they should look like it. Don't worry about them being perfectly shaped. They should be rustic, toothsome, and comforting—and that's perfect enough.

DUMPLINGS

Just as hearty stews hint at cold climates and fish dishes nod to coastal regions in any country, the dumplings of Italy reveal much about the lands from which they hail. If the dumpling includes bread crumbs, for example, it likely comes from the north, as a short growing season causes bread to be the main staple. Ricotta and potatoes as dumpling ingredients signal the rich pastures of the middle of the country. Semolina flour is common in the south, where the fields abound with durum wheat. It made sense to me, then, to organize the dumplings in this book by area, starting with the island of Sardinia, then moving to the southern part of Italy, up through the center, and concluding in the north. Within each area, the dumpling recipes are organized from easiest to more challenging to make.

In Italy, pasta and dumplings are traditionally the *primo* course of a meal, akin to an appetizer in the United States. Italians eat large portions of pasta, however, even as a starter; my serving suggestions are fit for either an Italian-size starter or an American-size main course. Italians serve fried dumplings such as Crescentina (page 115) only as starters, rarely as a *primo* course.

In terms of storage, uncooked potato gnocchi kept in the refrigerator for more than a couple of days tend to oxidize and turn spotty and dark, though they are still edible; for longer storage, they hold their freshness best when frozen. Freezing most types of uncooked dumplings helps them retain moisture and remain tender, but not all dumplings can be frozen; each recipe notes how best and how long to store them.

MALLOREDDUS

SERVES 10

Malloreddus are also known as gnocchetti Sardi, *which means "little Sardinian gnocchi." The shape of the pasta is similar to cavatelli, but the dough is made with semolina instead of finer wheat flour, giving the dumpling a sturdy and toothsome texture. Eggs are never included in malloreddus dough. Saffron gives a subtle flavor to the pasta and colors the dough bright yellow. At the height of the spice trade, saffron was so abundant it was essentially a peasant food. It was far less expensive than eggs, which were considered a luxury, and the spice was used liberally to mimic the richness and color of eggs. These wonderful dumplings are hearty and lightly scented of saffron.*

400 G/1¾ CUPS WATER

½ TSP SAFFRON THREADS

795 G/4½ CUPS + 2 TBSP SEMOLINA FLOUR, PLUS MORE AS NEEDED AND FOR DUSTING

2 TSP KOSHER SALT

1 TBSP EXTRA-VIRGIN OLIVE OIL

SAUCE OF YOUR CHOICE (SUGGESTIONS FOLLOW)

Bring the water to a boil over high heat. In a small bowl, steep the saffron in the boiling water for 10 minutes. In a large bowl or the bowl of a stand mixer fitted with a dough hook attachment, combine the semolina, salt, and olive oil.

Set a fine-mesh strainer over the large bowl. Pour the saffron water through the strainer into the bowl, pressing the threads with your fingers to extract as much flavor as possible. Discard the saffron threads. Knead with your hands or on medium speed for 10 minutes, until the dough is cohesive. Cover the dough with plastic wrap and let rest at room temperature for 1 hour.

Line two baking sheets with parchment paper and dust with semolina flour. Make sure your dough can be handled. If it's sticky, knead in more semolina, 1 tsp at a time. Cut off a chunk of dough about the width of two fingers and cover the rest with plastic wrap. Roll the chunk in semolina to lightly coat. On an unfloured work surface, use your hands to roll the chunk into a log ¼ in (6 mm) in diameter. Cut the log into ½-in (12-mm) pieces. With the side of your thumb, gently push each piece against a gnocchi board or the back of the tines of a fork, rolling and flicking the dough to make a curled shape with an indentation on one side and a ridged surface on the other. Put the malloreddus on the prepared baking sheets and shape the remaining dough. Make sure that the malloreddus don't touch or they will stick together.

(To store, refrigerate on the baking sheets, covered with plastic wrap, for up to 2 days, or freeze on the baking sheets and transfer to an airtight container. Use within 1 month. Do not thaw before cooking.)

Bring a large pot filled with generously salted water to a simmer over medium-high heat. Add the malloreddus and simmer until they float to the surface, 1 to 3 minutes. Simmer for 1 to 2 minutes more, until slightly al dente. Remove immediately with a slotted spoon and finish with your choice of sauce. Serve right away.

SAUCE PAIRINGS: *Traditionally, malloreddus are paired with Tomato Sauce (page 175), Lamb Ragù (page 184), or Beef Ragù (page 186).*

CICIONES

Ciciones are Sardinian dumplings that feature saffron, an ingredient brought to Sardinia by the Moors (or perhaps by the Spanish—there is robust debate among Italians about this). Similar to Malloreddus (page 26), these dumplings are made from semolina. The difference between the two is that eggs are added to ciciones dough, but never to malloreddus dough. These dumplings are labor-intensive, but the reward of eating them is well worth the effort. The texture is slightly denser than similar dumplings, which is a result of the semolina.

55 G/¼ CUP WATER
1 TSP SAFFRON THREADS
800 G/4½ CUPS + 3 TBSP SEMOLINA FLOUR, PLUS MORE AS NEEDED AND FOR DUSTING
8 EGGS
2 TSP EXTRA-VIRGIN OLIVE OIL
1 TSP KOSHER SALT
SAUCE OF YOUR CHOICE (SUGGESTIONS FOLLOW)

Bring the water to a boil over high heat. In a small bowl, steep the saffron in the boiling water for 10 minutes. In a large bowl or the bowl of a stand mixer fitted with a dough hook attachment, combine the semolina flour, eggs, olive oil, and salt.

Set a fine-mesh strainer over the large bowl. Pour the saffron water through the strainer into the bowl, pressing the threads with your fingers to extract as much flavor as possible. Discard the saffron threads. Knead with your hands or on medium speed for 5 minutes, scraping the sides of the bowl, until the dough is cohesive and sturdy and forms a mass that doesn't crack or crumble. If the dough is sticky, add more semolina 1 Tbsp at a time. Cover the dough with

plastic wrap and let rest at room temperature for 1 hour.

Line two baking sheets with parchment paper and dust with semolina. Cut off a chunk of dough about the width of two fingers and leave the rest covered with plastic wrap. On an unfloured work surface, use your hands to roll the chunk into a log about ¼ in (6 mm) in diameter. Cut the log into ¼-in (6-mm) pieces and, using your thumb and forefinger, roll them into balls, rounding out the edges so they look like chickpeas. Put the ciciones on the prepared baking sheets and shape the remaining dough. Make sure that the ciciones don't touch or they will stick together.

(To store, refrigerate on the baking sheets, covered with plastic wrap, for up to 2 days, or freeze on the baking sheets and transfer to an airtight container. Use within 1 month. Do not thaw before cooking.)

Bring a large pot filled with generously salted water to a simmer over medium-high heat. Add the ciciones and simmer until they float to the surface, 1 to 3 minutes. Simmer for 1 to 2 minutes more, until slightly al dente. Remove immediately with a slotted spoon and finish with your choice of sauce. Serve right away.

SAUCE PAIRINGS: *Traditionally, ciciones are paired with Tomato Sauce (page 175), Lamb Ragù (page 184), or Beef Ragù (page 186).*

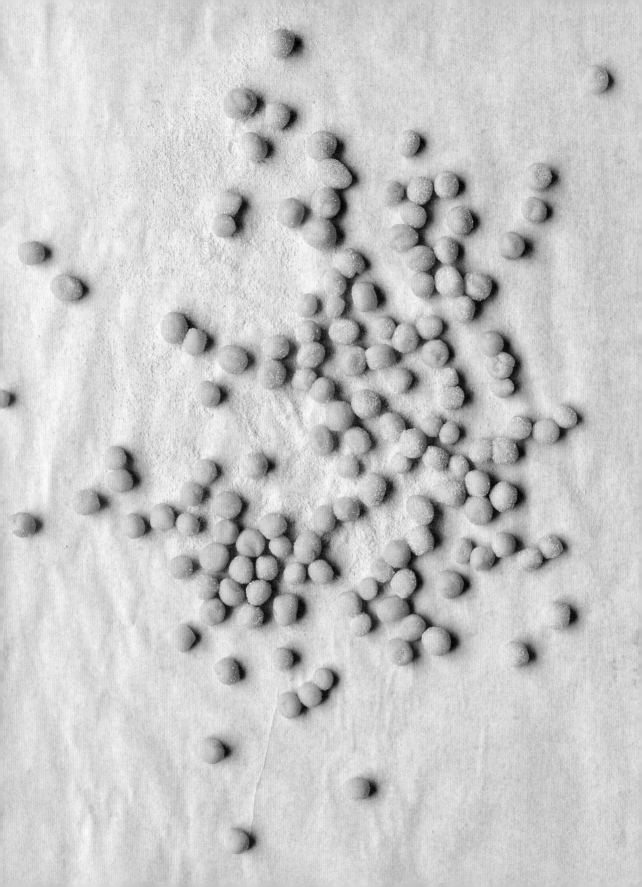

SEMOLINA CAVATELLI

SERVES 10

This recipe, featuring semolina, makes a sturdy dumpling. The texture is firmer and more toothsome than ricotta cavatelli, similar to malloreddus, which are also made from semolina, though the cavatelli are a little denser and made without any saffron. Semolina cavatelli pair well with sauces rooted in southern Italian staples, such as tomato, lamb, beef, and seafood.

400 G/1¾ CUPS WATER

865 G/5 CUPS SEMOLINA FLOUR, PLUS MORE FOR DUSTING

2 TSP KOSHER SALT

1 TBSP EXTRA-VIRGIN OLIVE OIL

SAUCE OF YOUR CHOICE (SUGGESTIONS FOLLOW)

Bring the water to a boil over high heat. In a large bowl or the bowl of a stand mixer fitted with a dough hook attachment, combine the semolina flour, boiling water, salt, and olive oil. Knead with your hands or on medium speed for 10 minutes, until fully combined and the dough is mostly smooth. Cover the dough with plastic wrap and let rest at room temperature for 30 minutes.

Line two baking sheets with parchment paper and dust with semolina. Cut off a chunk of dough about the width of two fingers and leave the rest covered with plastic wrap. On a work surface very lightly dusted with semolina, use your hands to roll the chunk into a log about ½ in (12 mm) in diameter. Do not incorporate too much more semolina into the dough, adding just enough so the dough does not stick to the surface. Cut the log into ½- to 1-in (12-mm to 2.5-cm) pieces. With the side of your thumb, gently push each piece against a gnocchi board or the back of the tines of a fork, rolling and flicking the dough to make a curled shape with an indentation on one side and a ridged surface on the other. Put the cavatelli on the prepared baking sheets and shape the remaining dough. Make sure that the cavatelli don't touch or they will stick together.

(To store, refrigerate on the baking sheets, covered with plastic wrap, for up to 2 days, or freeze on the baking sheets and transfer to an airtight container. Use within 1 month. Do not thaw before cooking.)

Bring a large pot filled with generously salted water to a simmer over medium-high heat. Add the cavatelli and simmer until they float to the surface, 1 to 3 minutes. Simmer for 1 to 2 minutes more, until al dente. Remove immediately with a slotted spoon and finish with your choice of sauce. Serve right away.

SAUCE PAIRINGS: *Traditionally, semolina cavatelli are paired with Tomato Sauce (page 175), Rabbit Ragù (page 182), Lamb Ragù (page 184), or Beef Ragù (page 186).*

RICOTTA CAVATELLI

SERVES 8

This Italian dumpling is one of the first I learned to make. One year, my husband bought me a hand-crank cavatelli machine for my birthday. We now use that machine at Lincoln, and it has been repaired and rewelded twice because it gets so much use! The recipe for ricotta cavatelli in the booklet that was included with the machine yields perfectly tender and flavorful dumplings; I have adapted that recipe to make hand-formed ricotta cavatelli that are equally delicious. If you own a hand-crank cavatelli machine, follow the manufacturer's instructions for forming the dumplings.

500 G/3½ CUPS + 1 TBSP ALL-PURPOSE FLOUR, PLUS MORE FOR DUSTING

1 TSP KOSHER SALT

480 G/2 CUPS WHOLE-MILK RICOTTA CHEESE, HOMEMADE (SEE PAGE 190) OR STORE-BOUGHT

55 G/¼ CUP WHOLE MILK

1 EGG

SAUCE OF YOUR CHOICE (SUGGESTIONS FOLLOW)

In a large bowl or the bowl of a stand mixer fitted with a dough hook attachment, combine the flour, salt, ricotta, milk, and egg. Knead with your hands or on medium speed for 10 minutes, until fully combined and the dough is mostly smooth. Cover the dough with plastic wrap and let rest at room temperature for 30 minutes.

Line two baking sheets with parchment paper and dust with flour. Cut off a chunk of dough about the width of two fingers and leave the rest covered with plastic wrap. On a lightly floured work surface, use your hands to roll the chunk into a log about ½ in (12 mm) in diameter. Do not incorporate too much more flour into the dough, adding just enough so the dough does not stick to the surface. Cut the log into ½- to 1-in (12-mm to 2.5-cm) pieces. With the side of your thumb, gently push each piece against

a gnocchi board or the back of the tines of a fork, rolling and flicking the dough to make a curled shape with an indentation on one side and a ridged surface on the other. Put the cavatelli on the prepared baking sheets and shape the remaining dough. Make sure that the cavatelli don't touch or they will stick together.

(To store, refrigerate on the baking sheets, covered with plastic wrap, for up to 2 days, or freeze on the baking sheets and transfer to an airtight container. Use within 1 month. Do not thaw before cooking.)

Bring a large pot filled with generously salted water to a simmer over medium-high heat. Add the cavatelli and simmer until they float to the surface, 1 to 3 minutes. Remove immediately with a slotted spoon and finish with your choice of sauce. Serve right away.

SAUCE PAIRINGS: *Traditionally, ricotta cavatelli are paired with Pesto (page 172); Tomato Sauce (page 175); Guanciale, Tomato, and Red Onion Sauce (page 176); Brown Butter with Sage (page 178); Fonduta (page 179); Gorgonzola Cream Sauce (page 180); Liver, Pancetta, and Porcini Ragù (page 181); Rabbit Ragù (page 182); Lamb Ragù (page 184); or Beef Ragù (page 186).*

ORECCHIETTE

Orecchiette are small, handmade pasta sometimes called "Puglian gnocchi." They fit into the category of pasta corta, or short pasta, but have the texture and weight of handmade dumplings. The old women in Bari Vecchia produce these dumplings, by hand, at an impressive speed; watching them is amazing. Sometimes the dough will be made with semolina and regular wheat flour, other times buckwheat flour or burned flour. In ancient times, burned flour was made by the poor from bits of wheat reaped from fields that were burned after the harvest. Traditionally, orecchiette are finished with sautéed turnip greens (see page 38) and topped with grated Parmigiano-Reggiano cheese.

255 G/1½ CUPS SEMOLINA FLOUR, PLUS MORE FOR DUSTING

255 G/1¾ CUPS + 1 TBSP ALL-PURPOSE FLOUR

2 TSP KOSHER SALT

255 G/1 CUP + 1 TBSP WARM WATER, PLUS MORE AS NEEDED

In a large bowl or the bowl of a stand mixer fitted with a dough hook attachment, combine the semolina flour, all-purpose flour, and salt at medium speed. Add the water and stir with a wooden spoon or mix on medium speed until a cohesive but not sticky dough forms, 1 to 2 minutes. Add more water, 1 Tbsp at a time, and knead with your hands or on medium speed until the dough is smooth and soft without being sticky or dry, about 8 minutes more. Cover the dough with plastic wrap and let rest at room temperature for 1 hour.

Line two baking sheets with parchment paper and dust with semolina. Cut off a chunk of dough about the width of two fingers and cover the rest with plastic wrap. On an unfloured work surface, use your hands to roll the chunk into a log about ¾ in (2 cm) in diameter. Cut the log into ¼-in (6-mm) pieces. Lightly dust the work surface with semolina. Press down on each piece of dough with your thumb, pushing away from you and twisting slightly to form an indented disk. Now place the disk on the tip of your thumb and gently pull down on the edges with your other fingers, molding the dough to form a cup shape. Put the orecchiette on the prepared baking sheets and shape the remaining dough. Make sure that the orecchiette don't touch or they will stick together.

(To store, refrigerate on the baking sheets, covered with plastic wrap, for up to 2 days, or freeze on the baking sheets and transfer to an airtight container. Use within 1 month. Do not thaw before cooking.)

Bring a large pot filled with generously salted water to a simmer over medium-high heat. Add the orecchiette and simmer until they float to the surface, 2 to 3 minutes. Simmer for 1 to 2 minutes more, until al dente. Remove immediately with a slotted spoon. Serve right away.

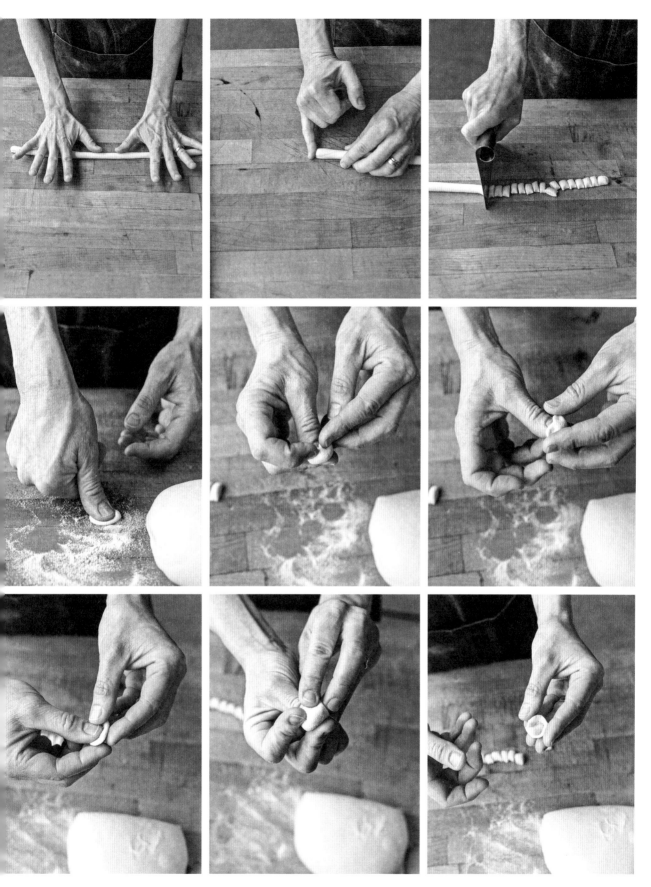

ORECCHIETTE WITH TURNIP GREENS, ANCHOVIES, AND GARLIC

SERVES 6

This is a typical dish in Puglia. If you cannot find turnip greens, mustard greens make a good substitute.

2¼ LB (1 KG) TURNIP GREENS, TOUGH RIBS REMOVED, TENDER RIBS AND LEAVES RESERVED

½ CUP (120 ML) EXTRA-VIRGIN OLIVE OIL

9 ANCHOVY FILLETS IN OIL

3 GARLIC CLOVES, MINCED

1 TO 1½ SMALL RED CHILES SUCH AS RED FRESNO, CHOPPED, OR ¼ TO ½ TSP RED PEPPER FLAKES

1½ TSP KOSHER SALT

1 RECIPE ORECCHIETTE (PAGE 36), JUST COOKED

PARMIGIANO-REGGIANO CHEESE FOR GRATING

Prepare an ice bath by filling a large bowl with ice and cold water. Bring a large pot filled with generously salted water to a boil over medium-high heat. Add the turnip leaves and tender ribs and blanch until tender, about 3 minutes. Drain the greens in a colander and transfer to the ice bath. When cool, drain again. Place the greens in a kitchen towel and wring until mostly dry. Coarsely chop the greens.

In a large sauté pan, warm the olive oil over medium-low heat. Add the anchovies, garlic, and chiles and sauté until the anchovies break apart, about 2 minutes. Add the turnip greens and sauté until the flavors meld, 5 to 6 minutes. Add the salt. Add the just-cooked orecchiette to the pan with the turnip greens. Cook for 2 minutes, stirring occasionally, until the orecchiette absorb the flavors of the sauce. Serve right away, topped with grated Parmigiano-Reggiano.

GNOCCHI ALLA SORRENTINA

SERVES 4

This is a hearty, rustic dish typical of the coastal village of Sorrento. A simple combination of gnocchi, tomato sauce, mozzarella, and fresh basil, it's Italian comfort food at its best.

1 RECIPE TOMATO SAUCE (PAGE 175)

1 RECIPE POTATO GNOCCHI (PAGE 78), JUST COOKED

8 OZ (225 G) FRESH MOZZARELLA CHEESE, CUT INTO ½-IN (12-MM) CUBES

8 LARGE FRESH BASIL LEAVES, TORN

KOSHER SALT

In a large sauté pan over medium heat, bring the tomato sauce to a bare simmer. Add the cooked gnocchi and mozzarella. Stir gently and cook just until heated through, about 30 seconds. Add the basil and season with salt. Serve right away.

DUNDERI

SERVES 4 TO 6

From the Amalfi Coast, these are light, delicate ricotta dumplings, sometimes made with lemon zest from the amazing local Amalfi citrus. They are held together with as little flour as possible to keep their texture creamy and tender. Somehow, Donderets (page 126), their cousins from Piedmont, have lost the ricotta and substituted potato instead.

480 G/2 CUPS WHOLE-MILK RICOTTA CHEESE, HOMEMADE (SEE PAGE 190) OR STORE-BOUGHT

6 EGG YOLKS

45 G/½ CUP GRATED PARMIGIANO-REGGIANO CHEESE

FRESHLY GRATED NUTMEG

1 TSP KOSHER SALT

160 G/1 CUP + 2 TBSP ALL-PURPOSE FLOUR, PLUS MORE FOR DUSTING

SEMOLINA FLOUR FOR DUSTING

SAUCE OF YOUR CHOICE (SUGGESTIONS FOLLOW)

In a large bowl, mix the ricotta and egg yolks until smooth. Add the Parmigiano-Reggiano cheese, a few swipes of nutmeg, the salt, and the all-purpose flour and mix with a wooden spoon just until the dough comes together.

Dust 30 g/¼ cup all-purpose flour on the work surface, then scrape the dough from the bowl directly on top of the flour. Sprinkle the top of the dough with an additional 30 g/¼ cup all-purpose flour. This will help prevent the dough from being too sticky to roll.

Line a baking sheet with parchment paper and dust with semolina flour. Cut off a chunk of dough about the width of two fingers and cover the rest with plastic wrap. On an unfloured work surface, use your hands to roll the chunk into a log about ½ in

(12 mm) in diameter. Cut the log into pieces ½ to 1 in (12 mm to 2.5 cm) long. Place the dunderi on the prepared baking sheet and shape the remaining dough. Make sure that the dunderi don't touch or they will stick together.

(To store, refrigerate on the baking sheet, covered with plastic wrap, for up to 2 days, or freeze on the baking sheet and transfer to an airtight container. Use within 1 month. Do not thaw before cooking.)

Bring a large pot filled with generously salted water to a simmer over medium-high heat. Add the dunderi and simmer until they float to the surface, 1 to 3 minutes. Remove immediately with a slotted spoon and finish with your choice of sauce. Serve right away.

SAUCE PAIRINGS: *Traditionally, dunderi are simply dressed with melted butter or Tomato Sauce (page 175).*

WINTER SQUASH CAVATELLI

SERVES 6

This tender squash dumpling is the perfect way to welcome fall and the long ride through winter. The flavor is earthy and sweet, pairing well with sage butter for a simple sauce or with Gorgonzola cream sauce for something richer. Squash cavatelli hails from Italy's newest region, Molise, which gained independence from Abruzzo in 1963. Many regions of Italy grow fall and winter squash varieties easily and, like potatoes, squash stores well when fresh produce is limited.

200 G/½ CUP + 5 TBSP SQUASH PURÉE (PAGE 191)

2 EGGS

170 G/1 CUP SEMOLINA FLOUR, PLUS MORE FOR DUSTING

230 G/1½ CUPS + 2 TBSP ALL-PURPOSE FLOUR, PLUS MORE FOR DUSTING

SAUCE OF YOUR CHOICE (SUGGESTIONS FOLLOW)

In a large bowl or the bowl of a stand mixer fitted with a dough hook attachment, combine the squash purée, eggs, semolina flour, and all-purpose flour. Knead with your hands or on medium speed for 10 minutes, until fully combined and the dough is mostly smooth. Cover the dough with plastic wrap and let rest at room temperature for 30 minutes.

Line two baking sheets with parchment paper and dust with semolina. Cut off a chunk of dough about the width of two fingers and leave the rest covered with plastic wrap. On a work surface lightly dusted with all-purpose flour, use your hands to roll the chunk into a log about ½ in (12 mm) in diameter. Do not incorporate too much more flour into the dough, adding just enough so the dough does not stick to the surface. Cut the log into ½- to 1-in (12-mm to 2.5-cm) pieces. With the side of your thumb, gently push each piece against a gnocchi board or the back of the tines of a fork, rolling and flicking the dough to make a curled shape with an indentation on one side and a ridged surface on the other. Put the cavatelli on the prepared baking sheets and shape the remaining dough. Make sure that the cavatelli don't touch or they will stick together.

(To store, refrigerate on the baking sheets, covered with plastic wrap, for up to 2 days, or freeze on the baking sheets and transfer to an airtight container. Use within 1 month. Do not thaw before cooking.)

Bring a large pot filled with generously salted water to a simmer over medium-high heat. Add the cavatelli and simmer until they float to the surface, 1 to 3 minutes. Remove immediately with a slotted spoon and finish with your choice of sauce. Serve right away.

SAUCE PAIRINGS: *Traditionally, winter squash cavatelli are paired with Brown Butter with Sage (page 178), Gorgonzola Cream Sauce (page 180), or Lamb Ragù (page 184).*

PASTA GRATTUGIATA

SERVES 6

Originally from Lazio, pasta grattugiata is an ancient and rustic preparation. The name literally translates as "grated pasta," and it is simple to make. The ingredients are inexpensive and, like many rustic Italian dishes, the dish was created by the poor to utilize old or stale bread. It is served in broth to make a very savory and satisfying dish. Some versions include a bit of freshly grated nutmeg. This deeply comforting soup is the Italian version of the chicken soup I grew up on.

50 G/¼ CUP + 3 TBSP DRIED BREAD CRUMBS
140 G/1 CUP "00" FLOUR (SEE PAGE 16)
2 EGGS
50 G/½ CUP + 1 TBSP GRATED PARMIGIANO-REGGIANO CHEESE
8 CUPS (2 L) CHICKEN STOCK (PAGE 189)
KOSHER SALT

In the bowl of a food processor, process the bread crumbs until finely ground. Add the flour, eggs, and Parmigiano-Reggiano cheese and process until a ball is formed, about 1 minute. Transfer to a work surface and knead the mixture with your hands 10 times, or until a cohesive dough forms. Cover with plastic wrap and let rest at room temperature for 30 minutes.

On the large holes of a box grater, grate the dough into small crumbles.

Fill a large pot with the chicken stock and bring to a simmer over medium heat. Add the pasta grattugiata and simmer until tender, about 2 minutes. Lightly season the broth with salt and serve right away.

GNOCCHI ALLA ROMANA

SERVES 6

This is a recipe from a friend of mine, Ethan Stowell. He is the chef and owner of a bunch of Italian-focused restaurants in Seattle. One of his restaurants, Rione XIII, is focused solely on Roman cuisine. While many gnocchi are cooked in simmering water, gnocchi alla romana—Roman gnocchi—are made from cooking semolina in milk, similar to making polenta, and later baking the dumplings in an oven, preferably a wood-fired one. Modern, health-conscious Italians are backing off from finishing the semolina with butter, using olive oil instead.

975 G/4 CUPS WHOLE MILK
170 G/1 CUP SEMOLINA FLOUR
4 EGG YOLKS
135 G/1½ CUPS GRATED PARMIGIANO-REGGIANO CHEESE
KOSHER SALT
FRESHLY GRATED NUTMEG
UNSALTED BUTTER FOR THE BAKING SHEET, PLUS 115 G/8 TBSP DICED

In a 4-qt (3.8-L) saucepan, bring the milk to a boil over medium-high heat. Turn the heat to low and add the semolina flour, pouring it in a steady stream and whisking constantly. Once the semolina has been whisked in and there are no lumps, switch to a wooden spoon and continue to stir for 2 minutes. Remove from the heat, stir in the egg yolks, one at a time, and then add half of the Parmigiano-Reggiano cheese. Season with salt and nutmeg.

Butter a baking sheet. Pour the semolina mixture onto the prepared baking sheet and smear to a thickness of about 1 in (2.5 cm). Let cool to room temperature, then cover with plastic wrap and refrigerate until cold and firm, preferably overnight.

Preheat the oven to 400°F (200°C). Use 2 Tbsp of the butter to grease a 9-by-13-in (23-by-33-cm) baking dish or six individual gratin dishes.

Using a 2-in (5-cm) round pastry cutter, cut out circles of dough. Arrange the circles in the buttered baking dish or gratin dishes, overlapping them slightly, and sprinkle with the remaining 85 g/6 Tbsp butter and the remaining Parmigiano-Reggiano, evenly dividing the butter and cheese if using individual dishes. (Gnocchi alla romana can be refrigerated for up to 3 days, covered with plastic wrap, before topping with butter and cheese and baking.) Bake until the butter and cheese are melted and the tops of the gnocchi are a rich golden brown, 10 to 15 minutes. Serve right away.

SEMOLINA FRASCARELLI

SERVES 6

Made with semolina, this version of frascarelli is tender and less toothy than many semolina-based dumplings. The dumplings are sturdy and easy to make; remarkably wonderful when you realize how few ingredients are needed to produce such a tasty dish. Make frascarelli with your children: semolina frascarelli come together quickly and simply and will teach your children that homemade food can be simple to make and gratifying to eat!

900 G/4 CUPS ICE WATER
910 G/5¼ CUPS + 2 TBSP SEMOLINA FLOUR
SAUCE OF YOUR CHOICE (SUGGESTIONS FOLLOW)

Line a baking sheet with parchment paper. Fill a bowl with the ice water.

Place half of the semolina flour on another baking sheet and spread it out evenly, leaving a rough 3-in (7.5-cm) border of the baking sheet uncovered. Dip one hand into the ice water and drip several large droplets from your fingers onto the semolina flour on the baking sheet. (Do not spray the water onto the flour because the droplets will be too small.) Use a metal bench scraper to turn the semolina flour over itself, creating small dough chunks about ¼ in (6 mm) in size. Using the bench scraper, transfer the semolina flour with the frascarelli bits to a medium-mesh sieve or strainer. Gently shake the sieve, allowing the unmoistened semolina flour to fall back onto the baking sheet. Put the frascarelli on the parchment-lined baking sheet. Do not overcrowd the frascarelli or they will stick together. Continue making frascarelli using the semolina flour that has been sifted out and the remaining ice water until very little semolina flour remains, then place the remaining half of the semolina flour on the baking sheet and repeat the process until all the semolina flour and water have been used.

(To store, refrigerate the frascarelli, covered with plastic wrap, for up to 3 days.)

Bring a large pot filled with generously salted water to a simmer over medium-high heat. Add the frascarelli and simmer until they float to the surface, 1 to 3 minutes. Remove immediately with a slotted spoon and finish with your choice of sauce. Serve right away.

SAUCE PAIRINGS: *Traditionally, frascarelli are paired with Tomato Sauce (page 175) or served in soup, similar in style to Pisarei e Faso (page 105).*

FRASCARELLI

All-purpose flour is finer than semolina, making this version of frascarelli more tender and delicate and a little more difficult to form than Semolina Frascarelli (page 48). Forming takes a little more patience, but the final result—a very tender and silky dumpling—is well worth the effort. The semolina-dusted baking sheet used for resting formed frascarelli in this recipe is imperative in making sure that the dumplings do not stick to one another.

SEMOLINA FLOUR FOR DUSTING
900 G/4 CUPS ICE WATER
1.4 KG/9¾ CUPS ALL-PURPOSE FLOUR
SAUCE OF YOUR CHOICE (SUGGESTIONS FOLLOW)

Line a baking sheet with parchment paper and dust with semolina flour. Fill a bowl with the ice water.

Place half of the all-purpose flour on another baking sheet and spread it out evenly, leaving a rough 3-in (7.5-cm) border of the baking sheet uncovered. Dip one hand into the ice water and drip several large droplets from your fingers onto the all-purpose flour on the baking sheet. (Do not spray the water onto the flour because the droplets will be too small.) Use a metal bench scraper to turn the flour over itself, creating small dough chunks about ¼ in (6 mm) in size. Using the bench scraper, transfer the flour with the frascarelli bits to a medium-mesh sieve or strainer. Gently shake the sieve, allowing the unmoistened flour to fall back onto the baking sheet. Put the frascarelli on the parchment-lined baking sheet. Do not overcrowd the frascarelli or they will stick together. Continue making frascarelli using the all-purpose flour that has been sifted out and the remaining ice water until very little flour remains, then place the remaining half of the all-purpose flour on the baking sheet and repeat the process until all the flour and water have been used.

(To store, refrigerate the frascarelli, covered with plastic wrap, for up to 3 days.)

Bring a large pot filled with generously salted water to a simmer over medium-high heat. Add the frascarelli and simmer until they float to the surface, 1 to 3 minutes. Remove immediately with a slotted spoon and finish with your choice of sauce. Serve right away.

SAUCE PAIRINGS: *Traditionally, frascarelli are cooked in a brothy soup or paired with Tomato Sauce (page 175), but I like to add a bit of cream to the tomato sauce before adding the frascarelli.*

GNOCCHI RICCI, SINGLE DOUGH METHOD

SERVES 6

There are two methods for making gnocchi ricci: a single dough method and a method that combines two doughs (see page 54). The single dough method is easier but is not a shortcut and yields a great dish.

465 G/3⅓ CUPS "00" FLOUR (SEE PAGE 16)
1½ TSP KOSHER SALT
4 EGGS
2 TBSP WATER, PLUS MORE AS NEEDED
SEMOLINA FLOUR FOR DUSTING
SAUCE OF YOUR CHOICE (SEE PAGE 55)

In a large bowl or the bowl of a stand mixer fitted with a dough hook attachment, combine the "00" flour, salt, and eggs. Knead with your hands or on medium speed until the flour is moistened but the mixture is still shaggy, about 2 minutes. Add the water and continue to knead for 5 to 6 minutes, until fully combined and the dough is mostly smooth. Add more water, 1 tsp at a time, if the dough is too dry to form a ball. Cover the dough with plastic wrap and let rest at room temperature for 1 hour.

Line two baking sheets with parchment paper and dust with semolina flour. Cut off a chunk of dough about the width of two fingers and cover the rest with plastic wrap. On an unfloured work surface, use your hands to roll the chunk into a log about ½ in (12 mm) in diameter. Cut the log into ½-in (12-mm) pieces. With your index and middle fingers, drag a piece across the work surface, creating an indentation in the center. With the index and middle fingers of one hand and the thumb of your other hand, gently stretch the piece, pressing it against the surface and pulling in opposite directions to create a slightly larger and flatter surface. The finished gnocchi will be slightly thicker around the edges, have irregular indentations in the center, and measure about 1½ in (4 cm) in size. Put the gnocchi on the prepared baking sheets and shape the remaining dough. Make sure that the gnocchi don't touch or they will stick together.

(To store, refrigerate on the baking sheets, covered with plastic wrap, for up to 2 days, or freeze on the baking sheets and transfer to an airtight container. Use within 1 month. Do not thaw before cooking.)

Bring a large pot filled with generously salted water to a simmer over medium-high heat. Add the gnocchi and simmer until they float to the surface, 1 to 3 minutes. Simmer until al dente, 2 to 3 minutes more. Remove immediately with a slotted spoon and finish with your choice of sauce. Serve right away.

GNOCCHI RICCI, DOUBLE DOUGH METHOD

SERVES 6

It's a mystery why two methods exist for making gnocchi ricci, but I have a theory. I think that back in the old days, a cook made gnocchi ricci but forgot to add an ingredient, so she made a second dough and incorporated it into the first. That resourcefulness turned into tradition.

500 G/3½ CUPS + 1 TBSP "00" FLOUR (SEE PAGE 16)
1½ TSP KOSHER SALT
4 EGGS
3 TBSP WATER, PLUS MORE AS NEEDED
SEMOLINA FLOUR FOR DUSTING
SAUCE OF YOUR CHOICE (SUGGESTIONS FOLLOW)

In a large bowl or the bowl of a stand mixer fitted with a dough hook attachment, combine 425 g/3 cups of the "00" flour, the salt, and the eggs. Knead with your hands or on medium speed for about 2 minutes, until a shaggy dough forms. Add 2 Tbsp of the water and continue to knead until the dough is fully combined and mostly smooth, about 6 minutes more. Add more water, 1 tsp at a time, if the dough is too hard and crumbly to come together. Pat the dough into a 5-in (12-cm) disk.

In a small bowl, mix the remaining 1 Tbsp water with the remaining 75 g/½ cup + 1 Tbsp "00" flour, until it forms a pliable paste. Pat the paste into a thin 5-in (12-cm) disk and lay it on top of the disk of dough. Gather up the sides and knead the disks together by hand until the dough and paste are fully incorporated and the mixture is smooth and cohesive, 3 to 4 minutes. Cover the dough with plastic wrap and let rest at room temperature for 1 hour.

Line two baking sheets with parchment paper and dust with semolina flour. Cut off a chunk of dough about the width of two fingers and cover the rest with plastic wrap. On an unfloured work surface, use your hands to roll the chunk into a log about ½ in (12 mm) in diameter. Cut the log into ½-in (12-mm) pieces. With your index and middle finger, drag a piece across your work surface, creating an indentation in the center. With your hands, gently stretch out the piece to create a slightly larger and flatter surface. The finished gnocchi will be slightly curly around the edges, about 1½ in (4 cm) in size, and flatter in the center. Put the gnocchi on the prepared baking sheets and shape the remaining dough. Make sure that the gnocchi don't touch or they will stick together.

(To store, refrigerate on the baking sheets, covered with plastic wrap, for up to 2 days, or freeze on the baking sheets and transfer to an airtight container. Use within 1 month. Do not thaw before cooking.)

Bring a large pot filled with generously salted water to a simmer over medium-high heat. Add the gnocchi and simmer until they float to the surface, 1 to 3 minutes. Simmer until al dente, 2 to 3 minutes more. Remove immediately with a slotted spoon and finish with your choice of sauce. Serve right away.

SAUCE PAIRINGS: *Traditionally, gnocchi ricci are paired with Lamb Ragù (page 184) or Beef Ragù (page 186).*

[LAZIO]

CECAMARITI

SERVES 4

The name cecamariti, *translated as "husband blinders," refers to husbands coming home for dinner and being "blinded" by this spectacular dish. Originally from Lazio, this dumpling is traditionally made with leftover yeast bread dough, an easy way to make a bread and a pasta dish from the same dough. The addition of the wine and yeast add depth to the flavor. If you don't cook them immediately, make sure to freeze your dumplings after forming, since the yeast will cause the dough to continue to rise.*

55 G/¼ CUP WHITE WINE

170 G/¾ CUP WARM WATER

1 TBSP + 1 TSP ACTIVE DRY YEAST

1 TBSP HONEY

1 TSP KOSHER SALT

1 TBSP EXTRA-VIRGIN OLIVE OIL

420 G/3 CUPS ALL-PURPOSE FLOUR, PLUS MORE FOR DUSTING

SEMOLINA FLOUR FOR DUSTING

SAUCE OF YOUR CHOICE (SUGGESTIONS FOLLOW)

In a large bowl or the bowl of a stand mixer fitted with a dough hook attachment, stir together the wine, warm water, and yeast until dissolved. Set aside until the yeast blooms and becomes foamy, about 10 minutes. Add the honey, salt, and olive oil and mix with your hands or on medium speed until combined. Add the all-purpose flour and knead with your hands or on medium speed for 5 minutes, until a soft and cohesive dough is formed. The dough should not be sticky, dry, or stiff. Lightly oil a large bowl and place the dough in the bowl. Cover loosely with plastic wrap and allow to rise for 1 hour.

Line a baking sheet with parchment paper and dust with semolina flour. Cut off a chunk of dough about the width of two fingers and leave the rest covered with plastic wrap. On an unfloured work surface, use your hands to roll the chunk into a log about ½ in (12 mm) in diameter, dusting lightly with all-purpose flour as needed to keep the dough from sticking to the surface. Cut the log into ½-in (12-mm) pieces and roll each piece back and forth with your hands until it forms a spindle shape that is 2 in (5 cm) long— the ends should be narrow and the center thicker. Put the cecamariti on the prepared baking sheet and shape the remaining dough. Make sure that the cecamariti don't touch or they will stick together.

CONTINUED

(To store, refrigerate on the baking sheet, covered with plastic wrap, for up to 2 days, or freeze on the baking sheet and transfer to an airtight container. Use within 1 month. Do not thaw before cooking.)

Bring a large pot filled with generously salted water to a simmer over medium-high heat. Add the cecamariti and simmer until they float to the surface, 1 to 3 minutes. Remove immediately with a slotted spoon and finish with your choice of sauce. Serve right away.

SAUCE PAIRINGS: *Traditionally, cecamariti are paired with Pesto (page 172); Tomato Sauce (page 175); Guanciale, Tomato, and Red Onion Sauce (page 176); Brown Butter with Sage (page 178); Fonduta (page 179); Gorgonzola Cream Sauce (page 180); Liver, Pancetta, and Porcini Ragù (page 181); Rabbit Ragù (page 182); Lamb Ragù (page 184); or Beef Ragù (page 186).*

CAZZELLITTI

SERVES 4

Cazzellitti *means "little hats," and these dumplings look similar to cavatelli. They are quite small and have a tiny groove that's made by dragging a butter knife across a small piece of dough. Caz-zellitti are a specialty of Abruzzo and are traditionally a rustic dumpling made by shepherds who live in very remote areas. They relied on foods that they could grow or gather, and the sauces for this dumpling tend to be made from simple seasonal greens or mutton. This dumpling is soft and tender.*

170 G/1 CUP SEMOLINA FLOUR, PLUS MORE FOR DUSTING

300 G/2 CUPS + 2 TBSP ALL-PURPOSE FLOUR, PLUS MORE FOR DUSTING

1 TBSP EXTRA-VIRGIN OLIVE OIL

1 TSP KOSHER SALT

110 G/½ CUP WARM WATER, PLUS MORE AS NEEDED

SAUCE OF YOUR CHOICE (SUGGESTIONS FOLLOW)

In a large bowl or the bowl of a stand mixer fitted with a dough hook attachment, combine the semolina flour and the all-purpose flour. Add the olive oil, salt, and water. Knead with your hands or on medium speed, adding more water, 1 Tbsp at a time, until the dough is soft and cohesive, about 5 minutes. The dough should not be sticky, dry, or stiff. Cover the dough with plastic wrap and let rest at room temperature for 1 hour.

Line a baking sheet with parchment paper and dust with semolina flour. Cut off a chunk of dough about the width of two fingers and cover the rest with plastic wrap. On a work surface lightly dusted with all-purpose flour, use your hands to roll the chunk into a log about ½ in (12 mm) in diameter. Do not incorporate too much more flour into the dough, adding just enough so the dough does not stick to the surface. Cut the log into ½-in (12-mm) pieces. Using the tip of a butter knife held at an angle to the work surface, gently press down on each piece and drag it across the surface so that the dough curls and forms a tightly rolled dumpling. Put the cazzellitti on the prepared baking sheet and shape the remaining dough. Make sure that the cazzellitti don't touch or they will stick together.

CONTINUED

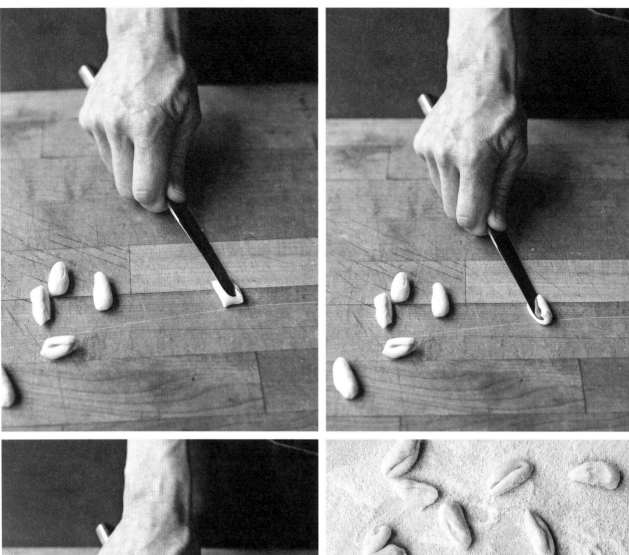

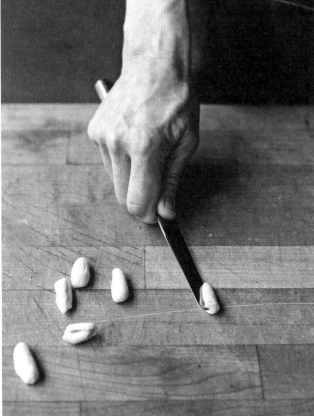

(To store, refrigerate on the baking sheet, covered with plastic wrap, for up to 2 days, or freeze on the baking sheet and transfer to an airtight container. Use within 1 month. Do not thaw before cooking.)

Bring a large pot filled with generously salted water to a simmer over medium-high heat. Add the cazzellitti and simmer until they float to the surface, 1 to 3 minutes. Remove immediately with a slotted spoon and finish with your choice of sauce. Serve right away.

SAUCE PAIRINGS: *Cazzellitti pair well with Lamb Ragù (page 184). They are also great when used in place of orecchiette in Orecchiette with Turnip Greens, Anchovies, and Garlic (page 38); omit the anchovies and top with grated aged Pecorino-Romano.*

SAFFRON AND POTATO GNOCCHI WITH GARLIC, RICOTTA, AND BUTTER SAUCE

SERVES 4

This wonderful recipe combines the weight and texture of durum flour with the tenderness of potatoes and the floral scent and flavor of saffron. Saffron has found its way up through many regions of Italy and is proudly grown in the Navelli plain in Abruzzo. I think this recipe is so special; the flavors and textures of the gnocchi paired with the ricotta and garlic sauce are unlike most gnocchi, which are usually served with a meat ragù or melted butter. Saffron and potato gnocchi are fragrant, rich, and decadent.

GNOCCHI

540 G/19 OZ RUSSET OR YUKON GOLD POTATOES

2 EGG YOLKS

1 TSP KOSHER SALT

LARGE PINCH OF SAFFRON THREADS

100 G/¾ CUP DURUM FLOUR (SEE PAGE 16)

SEMOLINA FLOUR FOR DUSTING

SAUCE

3 TBSP EXTRA-VIRGIN OLIVE OIL

1 GARLIC CLOVE, THINLY SLICED

½ TSP SAFFRON THREADS

KOSHER SALT

¼ CUP (60 G) WHOLE-MILK RICOTTA CHEESE, HOMEMADE (SEE PAGE 190) OR STORE-BOUGHT

3 TBSP UNSALTED BUTTER, AT ROOM TEMPERATURE

Make the gnocchi: In a medium pot, cover the potatoes with cold water. Bring the water to a simmer over medium-high heat and cook until the potatoes can be easily pierced with a skewer, 15 to 20 minutes. Drain the potatoes in a colander and set aside to cool.

When cool enough to handle, peel the potatoes and rice them into a large bowl.

Add the egg yolks, salt, saffron, and durum flour and mix by hand until the dough comes together. Transfer to a work surface and knead with your hands several times, until the dough is smooth and soft. Cover the dough with plastic wrap and let rest at room temperature for 30 minutes.

Line a baking sheet with parchment paper and dust with semolina flour. Cut off a chunk of dough about the width of two fingers and leave the rest covered with plastic wrap. On a work surface lightly dusted with semolina, use your hands to roll the chunk into a log about ½ in (12 mm) in diameter. Do not incorporate too much semolina into the dough, adding just enough so that the dough does not stick to the surface. Cut the log into ½- to 1-in (12-mm to 2.5-cm) pieces. Put the gnocchi on the prepared baking sheet and shape the remaining dough. Make sure that the gnocchi don't touch or they will stick together.

(To store, refrigerate on the baking sheet, covered with plastic wrap, for up to 2 days, or freeze on the baking sheet and transfer to an airtight container. Use within 1 month. Do not thaw before cooking.)

Bring a large pot filled with generously salted water to a simmer over medium-high heat.

Make the sauce: In a medium sauté pan, warm the olive oil over medium heat. Add the garlic and saffron and cook until the garlic is translucent, 4 to 5 minutes. If the garlic begins to brown, lower the heat. Remove from the heat and season lightly with salt. Add the ricotta cheese and butter; the sauce will look broken, as the ricotta, oil, and butter will not fully combine.

Add the gnocchi to the simmering water and cook until they float to the surface, 1 to 3 minutes. Remove immediately with a slotted spoon and add to the sauce. Toss to coat and serve right away.

FARRO GNOCCHI

Farro is a grain typical of Tuscany, though it has been introduced into most regions of Italy. I learned this recipe from Chef Federico Miglosi and his sous chef Giorgio Valiani in Umbria. The addition of the farro flour, a heavier flour, makes a slightly more dense gnocchi. The traditional ragù would be made from wild boar and, as Federico taught me, in Umbria the ragù is never finished with butter, only olive oil.

850 G/30 OZ RUSSET OR YUKON GOLD POTATOES
200 G/1½ CUPS ALL-PURPOSE FLOUR, PLUS MORE FOR DUSTING
200 G/¾ CUP FARRO FLOUR
2 EGGS
100 G/1 CUP + 1 TBSP FINELY GRATED PARMIGIANO-REGGIANO CHEESE
SEMOLINA FLOUR FOR DUSTING
SAUCE OF YOUR CHOICE (SUGGESTIONS FOLLOW)

In a medium pot, cover the potatoes with cold water. Bring the water to a simmer over medium-high heat and cook until the potatoes can be easily pierced with a skewer, 15 to 20 minutes. Drain the potatoes in a colander and set aside to cool.

When cool enough to handle, peel the potatoes and rice them into a large bowl. Add the all-purpose flour, farro flour, eggs, and Parmigiano-Reggiano cheese and mix by hand until the dough comes together. Transfer to a work surface and knead with your hands several times, until the dough is smooth and soft. Cover the dough with plastic wrap and let rest at room temperature for 30 minutes.

Line two baking sheets with parchment paper and dust with semolina flour. Cut off a chunk of dough about the width of two fingers and leave the rest covered with plastic wrap. On a work surface lightly dusted with all-purpose flour, use your hands to roll the chunk into a log about ½ in (12 mm) in diameter. Do not incorporate too much more flour into the dough, adding just enough so the dough does not stick to the surface. Cut the log into 1-in (2.5-cm) pieces. Put the gnocchi on the prepared baking sheets and shape the remaining dough. Make sure that the gnocchi don't touch or they will stick together.

(To store, refrigerate on the baking sheets, covered with plastic wrap, for up to 2 days, or freeze on the baking sheets and transfer to an airtight container. Use within 1 month. Do not thaw before cooking.)

Bring a large pot filled with generously salted water to a simmer over medium-high heat. Add the gnocchi and simmer until they float to the surface, 1 to 3 minutes. Remove immediately with a slotted spoon and finish with your choice of sauce. Serve right away.

SAUCE PAIRINGS: *Serve these gnocchi with Lamb Ragù (page 184) or Beef Ragù (page 186). Traditionally, gnocchi in Umbria are served with wild boar ragù. If you are able to get wild boar, you can substitute boar for the lamb in Lamb Ragù. Just braise for about 30 minutes longer, until the boar is very tender.*

GNOCCHI AL SAGRANTINO

SERVES 4 TO 6

This gnocchi comes from Montefalco, Umbria. I was wandering around this ancient town on a national holiday, the Monday after Easter, and the town was buzzing with Italians who had the day off. Strollers were being pushed, porchetta sandwiches were being sold on the piazza, and friends and families were relaxing outside on a semi-sunny day. Wandering back to the car, I passed a fresh pasta shop and stepped inside. It had all sorts of stuffed pastas and noodles, but this reddish gnocchi caught my eye. Silvia Sposini, the owner, explained that the local gnocchi was made with the local varietal of red wine, sagrantino. I asked for the recipe and she generously shared it with me. Then she reached into the case and packed up a generous amount for me to take away. Our hotel cooked them for us and served them with a simple sauce with sagrantino, guanciale, and a drizzle of honey. I sometimes use a rich red wine in the dough when making them Stateside, since sagrantino can be difficult to find. Any red that's not too light, fruity, or heavily oaked will do.

500 G/18 OZ RUSSET OR YUKON GOLD POTATOES

110 G/½ CUP SAGRANTINO OR OTHER RED WINE

2 TSP KOSHER SALT

200 G/1¼ CUPS + 3 TBSP ALL-PURPOSE FLOUR, PLUS MORE FOR DUSTING

1 EGG

SEMOLINA FLOUR FOR DUSTING

GUANCIALE, TOMATO, AND RED ONION SAUCE (PAGE 176)

In a medium pot, cover the potatoes with cold water. Bring the water to a simmer over medium-high heat and cook until the potatoes can be easily pierced with a skewer, 15 to 20 minutes. Drain the potatoes in a colander and set aside to cool.

When cool enough to handle, peel the potatoes and rice them into a large bowl. Add the wine, salt, all-purpose flour, and egg and mix by hand until the dough comes together. Transfer to a work surface and knead with your hands several times, until the dough is smooth and soft. Cover the dough with plastic wrap and let rest at room temperature for 30 minutes.

Line a baking sheet with parchment paper and dust with semolina flour. Cut off a chunk of dough about the width of two fingers and leave the rest covered with plastic wrap. On a work surface lightly dusted with all-purpose flour, use your hands to roll the chunk into a log about ½ in (12 mm) in diameter. Do not incorporate too much more flour into the dough; add just enough so that the dough does not stick to the surface. Cut the log into ½- to 1-in (12-mm to 2.5-cm) pieces.

Put the gnocchi on the prepared baking sheet and shape the remaining dough. Make sure that the gnocchi don't touch or they will stick together.

(To store, refrigerate on the baking sheet, covered with plastic wrap, for up to 2 days, or freeze on the baking sheet and transfer to an airtight container. Use within 1 month. Do not thaw before cooking.)

Bring a large pot filled with generously salted water to a simmer over medium-high heat. Add the gnocchi and simmer until they float to the surface, 1 to 3 minutes. Remove immediately with a slotted spoon and finish with the sauce. Serve right away.

GNOCCHI ALLA COLLESCIPOLANA

SERVES 6

This rustic gnocchi is a tradition of the village Collescipoli. Like many culinary customs in Italy, this recipe was on the verge of becoming lost. Thanks to the elder women of the village teaching much of the younger generation how to prepare this special, hearty dish, the ritual has continued.

GNOCCHI

100 G/¾ CUP + 1 TBSP DRIED BREAD CRUMBS
200 G/1¼ CUPS + 3 TBSP ALL-PURPOSE FLOUR, PLUS MORE FOR DUSTING
200 G/¾ CUP + 2 TBSP WARM WATER
SEMOLINA FLOUR FOR DUSTING

2 TBSP EXTRA-VIRGIN OLIVE OIL, PLUS MORE FOR DRIZZLING
2 GARLIC CLOVES, THINLY SLICED
1 CARROT, CUT INTO SMALL DICE
1 STALK CELERY, CUT INTO SMALL DICE
1 FRESH SAGE LEAF
¼ TSP RED PEPPER FLAKES
5¼ OZ (150 G) MILD PORK SAUSAGE, CASING REMOVED
3½ OZ (100 G) PANCETTA OR BACON, CUT INTO ¼-IN (6-MM) PIECES
KOSHER SALT
1 CUP (200 G) TOMATO PURÉE
1 CUP (200 G) COOKED BORLOTTI BEANS OR CANNELLINI BEANS
AGED PECORINO CHEESE FOR GRATING

Make the gnocchi: In the bowl of a food processor, process the bread crumbs until finely ground.

In a medium bowl, combine the bread crumbs and all-purpose flour. Add the warm water, 1 Tbsp at a time, and mix with your hands until a soft dough is formed. Cover the dough with plastic wrap and let rest at room temperature for 30 minutes.

Line two baking sheets with parchment paper and dust with semolina flour. Cut off a chunk of dough about the width of two fingers and cover the rest with plastic wrap. On a work surface lightly dusted with all-purpose flour, use your hands to roll the chunk into a log about ½ in (12 mm) in diameter. Cut the log into ¼-in (6-mm) pieces. Put the gnocchi on the prepared baking sheets and shape the remaining dough. Make sure that the gnocchi don't touch or they will stick together.

In a medium sauté pan, warm the olive oil over medium heat. Add the garlic, carrot, celery, sage, and red pepper flakes and sauté until the vegetables are tender, 4 to 5 minutes. Add the sausage and pancetta and sauté until the meat is cooked through, 3 to 4 minutes. Lightly season with salt, then add the tomato purée and beans. Turn the heat to low, and cook, stirring occasionally, until the sauce thickens and is not soupy, 15 to 20 minutes.

Bring a large pot filled with generously salted water to a simmer over medium-high heat. Add the gnocchi and simmer until they float to the surface, 1 to 3 minutes. Remove immediately with a slotted spoon and add to the sauce. Cook until the gnocchi absorb the sauce, 1 to 2 minutes. Add 1 to 2 Tbsp of the gnocchi cooking water if the sauce is dry. Season lightly with salt and drizzle with olive oil. Top with grated aged pecorino cheese and serve right away.

SORCETTI

Several years ago, I cooked for Alfredo, a local wine maker in Portland. We paired his pinot noir with sorcetti and lamb ragù. His family was originally from the Marche and whenever we served them sorcetti, he was delighted. He told me, "Where I come from, these are what grandmothers make for their grandchildren!" Sorcetti are a particularly rustic form of potato dumplings in which the potatoes are not fully puréed, creating a wonderfully unique texture. This is a peasant dish that is traditionally served with a thin mutton sauce. At Lincoln, we serve sorcetti with lamb ragù, which is much richer than the mutton sauce, and these wonderful dumplings deserve it.

455 G/1 LB MUSTARD GREENS, STEMMED

480 G/17 OZ RUSSET OR YUKON GOLD POTATOES, PEELED AND CUT INTO 1-IN (2.5-CM) CUBES

2 EGGS

KOSHER SALT

70 G/½ CUP ALL-PURPOSE FLOUR, PLUS MORE FOR DUSTING

SEMOLINA FLOUR FOR DUSTING

LAMB RAGÙ (PAGE 184)

Prepare an ice bath by filling a large bowl with ice and cold water. Bring a large pot filled with generously salted water to a boil over medium-high heat. Add the greens and blanch until wilted, about 1 minute. Remove immediately from the pot with tongs and transfer to the ice bath. When cool, drain the greens in a colander. Place the greens in a kitchen towel and wring until mostly dry. Finely chop and set aside.

In a medium pot, cover the potatoes with cold water. Bring the water to a simmer over medium-high heat and cook until the potatoes can be easily pierced with a skewer but are not falling apart, 15 to 20 minutes. Drain the potatoes in a colander and let sit for a few minutes to expel any additional moisture.

In a medium bowl, mash the potatoes coarsely with a whisk; there should not be any potato pieces larger than a pea. Allow to cool just long enough so that the potatoes can be handled. Add the greens and eggs, season with salt, and stir with a wooden spoon to combine. Add the all-purpose flour and mix by hand until the dough comes together. Transfer to a work surface and knead with your hands several times, until the dough is soft and sticky. Do not overknead or your sorcetti will be dense and pasty.

Dust 70 g/½ cup all-purpose flour on the work surface, then scrape the dough from the bowl on top of the flour. Sprinkle the top of the dough with 2 Tbsp all-purpose flour. This will help prevent the dough from being too sticky to roll.

Line two baking sheets with parchment paper and dust with semolina flour. Cut off a chunk of dough about the width of two fingers and cover the rest with plastic wrap. On a work surface lightly dusted with all-purpose flour, use your hands to roll the chunk into a log about ½ in (12 mm) in diameter. Do not incorporate too much more flour into the dough; add just enough so the dough does not stick to the surface. Cut the log into ½- to 1-in (12-mm to 2.5-cm) pieces. If any pieces of potato larger than a pea remain, remove and discard them. Put the sorcetti on the prepared baking sheets and shape the remaining dough. Make sure that the sorcetti don't touch or they will stick together.

Refrigerate on the baking sheets, uncovered, for 1 to 2 hours. Then use a metal bench scraper to flip the sorcetti. Dust with all-purpose flour, making sure the sorcetti do not stick to the parchment paper. Refrigerate for an additional 1 to 2 hours. The all-purpose flour will give the sorcetti a denser, noodle-like texture on the outside.

(To store, refrigerate on the baking sheets, covered with plastic wrap, for up to 2 days, or freeze on the baking sheets and transfer to an airtight container. Use within 1 month. Do not thaw before cooking.)

Bring another large pot filled with generously salted water to a simmer over medium-high heat. Add the sorcetti and simmer until they float to the surface, 1 to 3 minutes. Remove immediately with a slotted spoon and finish with the ragù. Serve right away.

STROZZAPRETI

In most of Italy, these dumplings are called gnocchi verdi *(gnocchi with greens) and* ricotta *or* ravioli gnudi *("nude ravioli," or ravioli filling without pasta). In Florence, they are called* strozza-preti, *or "priest stranglers." The story goes that a gluttonous priest, who loved these dumplings, ate so many of them so fast that he strangled himself by swallowing them whole. True story or not, these are some of my favorite dumplings. Don't worry, eat slowly and chew them well, and you will be fine.*

340 G/¾ LB LACINATO KALE OR WHITE CHARD, RIBS REMOVED

15 G/5 TBSP FRESH BREAD CRUMBS

2 EGGS

285 G/1 CUP + 2 TBSP WHOLE-MILK RICOTTA CHEESE, HOMEMADE (SEE PAGE 190) OR STORE-BOUGHT

100 G/1 CUP + 1 TBSP FINELY GRATED PARMIGIANO-REGGIANO CHEESE, PLUS MORE FOR SERVING

FRESHLY GRATED NUTMEG

KOSHER SALT AND GROUND BLACK PEPPER

ALL-PURPOSE FLOUR FOR DUSTING

2 TO 3 TBSP UNSALTED BUTTER, MELTED

Prepare an ice bath by filling a large bowl with ice and cold water. Bring a large pot filled with generously salted water to a boil over medium-high heat. Add the kale and blanch until tender, about 3 minutes. Remove immediately from the pot with tongs and transfer to the ice bath. When cool, drain the greens in a colander. Place the greens in a kitchen towel and wring until mostly dry. Finely chop and set aside.

In the bowl of a food processor, process the bread crumbs until finely ground. Add the kale, eggs, ricotta cheese, Parmigiano-Reggiano cheese, and a few swipes of nutmeg and process until well combined. Season with salt and pepper. Scrape the mixture into a bowl.

Line two baking sheets with parchment paper and dust with flour. Scoop a heaping spoonful of the ricotta mixture with one tea-spoon, and push it onto a prepared baking sheet with the back of a second teaspoon. With your hands, gently roll the strozzapreti around in the flour to coat. Repeat with the remaining dough. Make sure that the strozzapreti don't touch or they will stick together.

(To store, refrigerate on the baking sheets, uncovered, for up to 2 days. Do not freeze strozzapreti.)

Bring another large pot filled with generously salted water to a simmer over medium-high heat. Add the strozzapreti and simmer until they float to the surface, 1 to 3 minutes. Make sure to keep the cooking water at a simmer, as a rapid boil can break apart the strozzapreti. Remove immediately with a slotted spoon to a serving platter or individual bowls. Drizzle with the melted butter and top with grated Parmigiano-Reggiano. Serve right away.

RICOTTA GNOCCHETTI
SERVES 6

These gnocchetti are soft, tender, and rich with ricotta. In the fall, I dress them with sautéed squash and sage brown butter. In the winter, I serve them with a meat ragù. In the summer, it must be pesto!

480 G/2 CUPS WHOLE-MILK RICOTTA CHEESE, HOMEMADE (SEE PAGE 190) OR STORE-BOUGHT

25 G/¼ CUP FINELY GRATED PARMIGIANO-REGGIANO CHEESE

1 EGG

1 TBSP UNSALTED BUTTER, MELTED

FRESHLY GRATED NUTMEG

125 G/¾ CUP + 2 TBSP ALL-PURPOSE FLOUR, PLUS MORE FOR DUSTING

SEMOLINA FLOUR FOR DUSTING

SAUCE OF YOUR CHOICE (SUGGESTIONS FOLLOW)

In a large bowl, combine the ricotta cheese, Parmigiano-Reggiano cheese, egg, melted butter, and a few swipes of nutmeg. Add the all-purpose flour and mix with your hands just until combined. The dough should be slightly sticky and wet. Do not overmix, as this will make the gnocchetti tough.

Dust 30 g/¼ cup all-purpose flour on the work surface, then scrape the dough from the bowl directly on top of the flour. Sprinkle the top of the dough with an additional 30 g/ ¼ cup all-purpose flour. This will help prevent the dough from being too sticky to roll.

Line two baking sheets with parchment paper and dust with semolina flour. Cut off a chunk of dough, about 25 g/¼ cup, and cover the rest with plastic wrap. On a work surface lightly dusted with all-purpose flour, use your hands to roll the chunk into a log about ¼ in (6 mm) in diameter. Cut the log into ½-in (12-mm) pieces. Put the gnocchetti on the prepared baking sheets and shape the remaining dough. Make sure that the gnocchetti don't touch or they will stick together.

(To store, refrigerate on the baking sheets, covered with plastic wrap, for up to 2 days, or freeze on the baking sheets and transfer to an airtight container. Use within 1 month. Do not thaw before cooking.)

Bring a large pot filled with generously salted water to a simmer over medium-high heat. Add the gnocchetti and simmer until they float to the surface, 1 to 3 minutes. Remove immediately with a slotted spoon and finish with your choice of sauce. Serve right away.

SAUCE PAIRINGS: *Traditionally, ricotta gnocchetti are paired with Pesto (page 172); Tomato Sauce (page 175); Guanciale, Tomato, and Red Onion Sauce (page 176); Brown Butter with Sage (page 178); Liver, Pancetta, and Porcini Ragù (page 181); Rabbit Ragù (page 182); Lamb Ragù (page 184); or Beef Ragù (page 186).*

POTATO GNOCCHI

SERVES 4

Potato gnocchi are served throughout Italy, though traditionally they belong to the regional cuisine of central and northern Italy. And while I could have placed this recipe in many regional sections of this book, Tuscany was the first place in Italy where I ate gnocchi.

In Rome and Trento, Thursday is gnocchi day, during which many restaurants serve potato dumplings with a sauce or two for lunch and dinner. Some cooks swear that the best potatoes to use are the starchy potatoes that have been cellared all summer and into the winter. They tend to be softer because they have lost some of their water content, and much of the starch has turned to sugar. Like all potato-based gnocchi, when they are properly made, these dumplings will be light and tender.

400 G/14 OZ RUSSET OR YUKON GOLD POTATOES
75 G/½ CUP + 1 TBSP ALL-PURPOSE FLOUR, PLUS MORE FOR DUSTING
2 TSP KOSHER SALT
SEMOLINA FLOUR FOR DUSTING
SAUCE OF YOUR CHOICE (SUGGESTIONS FOLLOW)

In a medium pot, cover the potatoes with cold water. Bring the water to a simmer over medium-high heat and cook until the potatoes can be easily pierced with a skewer, 15 to 20 minutes. Drain the potatoes in a colander and set aside to cool.

When cool enough to handle, peel the potatoes and rice them into a bowl. Add the all-purpose flour and salt and stir with a wooden spoon until the dough comes together. Transfer to a work surface and knead with your hands several times, until the dough is smooth and soft. Cover the dough with plastic wrap and let rest at room temperature for 30 minutes.

Line a baking sheet with parchment paper and dust with semolina flour. Cut off a chunk of dough about the width of two fingers and leave the rest covered with plastic wrap. On a work surface lightly dusted with all-purpose flour, use your hands to roll the chunk into a log about ½ in (12 mm) in diameter. Do not incorporate too much more flour into the dough, adding just enough so the dough does not stick to the surface. Cut the log into ½- to 1-in (12-mm to 2.5-cm) pieces. With the side of your thumb, gently push each piece against a gnocchi board or the back of the tines of a fork, rolling and flicking the dough to make a curled shape with an indentation on one side and a ridged surface on the other. Put the gnocchi on the prepared baking sheet and shape the remaining dough. Make sure that the gnocchi don't touch or they will stick together.

(To store, refrigerate on the baking sheet, covered with plastic wrap, for up to 2 days, or freeze on the baking sheet and transfer to an airtight container. Use within 1 month. Do not thaw before cooking.)

Bring a large pot filled with generously salted water to a simmer over medium-high heat. Add the gnocchi and simmer until they float to the surface, 1 to 3 minutes. Remove immediately with a slotted spoon and finish with your choice of sauce. Serve right away.

SAUCE PAIRINGS: *Traditionally, potato gnocchi are paired with Pesto (page 172); Tomato Sauce (page 175); Guanciale, Tomato, and Red Onion Sauce (page 176); Brown Butter with Sage (page 178); Fonduta (page 179); Gorgonzola Cream Sauce (page 180); Liver, Pancetta, and Porcini Ragù (page 181); Rabbit Ragù (page 182); Lamb Ragù (page 184); or Beef Ragù (page 186).*

WILD NETTLE GNOCCHI

SERVES 4

Wild nettle, or ortica *in Italian, is a favorite springtime ingredient in Italy. This gnocchi concentrates the earthy and nutty flavor of wild nettles into bite-size dumplings that need no more than a little melted butter as a sauce. Often served in Tuscany, nettle dumplings are common throughout many regions of Italy. When wild nettles are available in the spring, the best place to find them is at a farmers' market; they are not widely available at stores. Nettles are very prickly (they are also known as stinging nettles), so use gloves when handling them raw. Once they are blanched, the leaves are no longer prickly and can be handled with bare hands once cooled.*

2 TBSP UNSALTED BUTTER, PLUS 2 TO 3 TBSP MELTED

115 G/½ CUP WATER

140 G/5 OZ WILD NETTLES, STEMMED

2 EGGS, PLUS 1 EGG YOLK

300 G/10½ OZ RUSSET OR YUKON GOLD POTATOES

165 G/1 CUP + 2 TBSP ALL-PURPOSE FLOUR, PLUS MORE AS NEEDED AND FOR DUSTING

1 TSP KOSHER SALT

PARMIGIANO-REGGIANO CHEESE FOR GRATING

In a large sauté pan, melt the 2 Tbsp butter with the water over medium heat. Add the nettles and cook until tender, about 5 minutes. Let cool completely in the pan. Place the nettles in a kitchen towel, wring until dry, and finely chop them. In a blender, process the nettles, eggs, and egg yolk, stopping occasionally to scrape down the sides of the blender bowl with a rubber spatula. Blend until the mixture forms a thick, cohesive paste.

In a medium pot, cover the potatoes with cold water. Bring the water to a simmer over medium-high heat and cook until the potatoes can be easily pierced with a skewer, 15 to 20 minutes. Drain the potatoes in a colander and set aside to cool.

When cool enough to handle, peel the potatoes and rice them into a large bowl. Add the nettle mixture and mix with a wooden spoon until combined. Add the flour and salt and knead with your hands until the dough comes together. The dough should be soft but not sticky. Add more flour, 1 Tbsp at a time, as needed, to achieve this texture.

Dust 30 g/¼ cup of flour on the work surface, then scrape the dough from the bowl directly on top of the flour. Sprinkle the top of the dough with an additional 30 g/¼ cup flour. This will help prevent the dough from being too sticky to roll.

Line a baking sheet with parchment paper and dust with flour. Cut off a chunk of dough about the width of two fingers and cover the rest with plastic wrap. On a lightly floured work surface, use your hands to roll the chunk into a log about ½ in (12 mm) in diameter. Do not incorporate too much more flour into the dough; add just enough so the dough does not stick to the surface. Cut the log into ½- to 1-in (12-mm to 2.5-cm) pieces. Put the gnocchi on the prepared baking sheet and shape the remaining dough. Make sure that the gnocchi don't touch or they will stick together.

(To store, refrigerate on the baking sheet, covered with plastic wrap, for up to 2 days, or freeze on the baking sheet and transfer to an airtight container. Use within 1 month. Do not thaw before cooking.)

Bring a large pot filled with generously salted water to a simmer over medium-high heat. Add the gnocchi and simmer until they float to the surface, 1 to 3 minutes. Remove immediately with a slotted spoon to a serving platter or four individual bowls. Drizzle with the melted butter and top with grated Parmigiano-Reggiano cheese. Serve right away.

PINCI

SERVES 6

This rustic pasta is always handmade, and it is traditionally almost the thickness of a pencil. The density of the noodle and the bite in its texture qualify pinci for the dumpling category. The exact length and thickness of pinci will vary, depending on village traditions or a family's preference. In some parts of Tuscany, the "n" is dropped and the pasta is called pici. *In Umbria, a similar pasta is called* stringozzi, *and in Lazio, it is called* umbricelli. *What I really love about this dumpling is its weight and chew. Pinci have an old-world feel that is unmistakably Italian.*

255 G/1½ CUPS SEMOLINA FLOUR, PLUS MORE FOR DUSTING

255 G/1¾ CUPS + 2 TBSP ALL-PURPOSE FLOUR

2 TSP SALT

255 G/1 CUP + 1 TBSP WARM WATER, PLUS MORE AS NEEDED

SAUCE OF YOUR CHOICE (SUGGESTIONS FOLLOW)

In a large bowl or the bowl of a stand mixer fitted with a dough hook attachment, combine the semolina flour, all-purpose flour, and salt at medium speed. Add the water and stir with a wooden spoon or mix on medium speed until a cohesive but not sticky dough forms, 1 to 2 minutes. Add more water, 1 Tbsp at a time, and knead with your hands or on medium speed until the dough is smooth and soft without being sticky or dry, about 8 minutes more. Cover the dough with plastic wrap and let rest at room temperature for 1 hour.

Line two baking sheets with parchment paper and dust with semolina flour. With a rolling pin, roll the dough on an unfloured work surface into a flat sheet ⅛ in (4 mm) thick, and then cut into ⅛-in- (4-mm-) wide strips. With your hands, roll one strip back and forth on the work surface into a fat spaghetti-like strand. Put the pinci on the prepared baking sheets and shape the remaining dough. Make sure that the pinci don't touch or they will stick together.

(To store, refrigerate on the baking sheets, covered with plastic wrap, for up to 2 days, or freeze on the baking sheets and transfer to an airtight container. Use within 1 month. Do not thaw before cooking.)

Bring a large pot filled with generously salted water to a simmer over medium-high heat. Add the pinci and simmer until they float to the surface, 1 to 3 minutes. Simmer until slightly al dente, 1 to 2 minutes more. Remove immediately with tongs and finish with your choice of sauce. Serve right away.

SAUCE PAIRINGS: *Traditionally, pinci are paired with heartier sauces such as Tomato Sauce (page 175); Liver, Pancetta, and Porcini Ragù (page 181); Rabbit Ragù (page 182); Lamb Ragù (page 184); or Beef Ragù (page 186).*

RUSTIC MALFATTI

SERVES 4

These tender dumplings typify Italian simplicity: quality ingredients and just a few steps make for a delicious dish. Each ingredient shines through with clarity. The spinach lends earthiness, while the eggs create richness. A simple coating of melted butter brings a soft sweetness to the dish. In this method, the dough is gently dropped into simmering water by the spoonful and poached.

910 G/2 LB FRESH SPINACH, STEMMED

4 EGGS

2 TSP KOSHER SALT

180 G/1¼ CUPS + 1 TBSP ALL-PURPOSE FLOUR

SAUCE OF YOUR CHOICE (SUGGESTIONS FOLLOW)

Prepare an ice bath by filling a large bowl with ice and cold water. Bring a large pot filled with generously salted water to a boil over medium-high heat. Add the spinach and blanch until wilted, about 2 minutes. Remove immediately from the pot with tongs and transfer to the ice bath. When cool, drain the spinach in a colander. Place the spinach in a kitchen towel and wring until mostly dry; a bit of residual moisture is fine.

Set a medium-mesh strainer over a large bowl. In a blender or food processor, process the eggs and spinach until smooth. Strain the spinach-egg mixture into the bowl. Discard the solids left in the strainer.

Add the salt and flour to the strained spinach-egg mixture, gently folding with a rubber spatula until the dough is cohesive and has the consistency of thick pancake batter.

(To store, refrigerate, in a bowl covered with plastic wrap, for up to 1 day. Do not freeze malfatti.)

Bring another large pot filled with generously salted water to a simmer over medium-high heat. Using two tablespoons, drop dollops of dough into the simmering water and cook until the malfatti float to the surface, 1 to 3 minutes. Remove immediately with a slotted spoon and finish with your choice of sauce. Serve right away.

SAUCE PAIRINGS: *Rustic malfatti pair best with melted butter or Tomato Sauce (page 175).*

FORMED MALFATTI

SERVES 6

In this recipe, malfatti dough is gently formed into balls, rolled in semolina flour, and rested in all-purpose flour. As the moisture from the filling dampens the flour, a tender noodle-like layer is formed. This is the closest to pasta ripiena—or filled pasta such as ravioli—that I have found in my research. It is one of my favorites and it's especially good when made with fresh, homemade ricotta.

500 G/18 OZ SWISS CHARD, RIBS REMOVED

480 G/2 CUPS WHOLE-MILK RICOTTA CHEESE, HOMEMADE (SEE PAGE 190) OR STORE-BOUGHT

4 EGGS

FRESHLY GRATED NUTMEG

30 G/⅓ CUP FINELY GRATED PARMIGIANO-REGGIANO CHEESE

KOSHER SALT AND FRESHLY GROUND BLACK PEPPER

70 G/½ CUP ALL-PURPOSE FLOUR, PLUS MORE FOR DUSTING

70 G/⅓ CUP + 2 TBSP SEMOLINA FLOUR

BROWN BUTTER WITH SAGE (PAGE 178)

Prepare an ice bath by filling a large bowl with ice and cold water. Bring a large pot filled with generously salted water to a boil over medium-high heat. Add the Swiss chard and blanch until tender, 3 to 4 minutes. Remove immediately from the pot with tongs and transfer to the ice bath. When cool, drain the chard in a colander, then place the chard in a kitchen towel and wring until very dry; make sure there is no excess moisture. Finely chop and set aside.

In a large bowl or the bowl of a stand mixer fitted with a paddle attachment, combine the ricotta cheese, eggs, a few swipes of nutmeg, and the Parmigiano-Reggiano cheese. Mix with your hands or on medium speed just until a dough forms. Mix in the greens just until combined and season with salt and pepper. Add the all-purpose flour and mix just until combined. Cover the bowl with plastic wrap and refrigerate for 30 minutes.

Line two baking sheets with parchment paper and dust very generously with all-purpose flour. Remove the dough from the refrigerator and gently stir to make sure any moisture that has settled in the bottom of the bowl is incorporated back into the mixture.

Put the semolina flour in a small bowl. Using a tablespoon, scoop out the dough and gently roll each scoop into a ball; it should be about the size of a walnut. Working with one ball at a time, gently roll in the semolina to lightly coat. Put the malfatti on the prepared baking sheets and shape the remaining dough. When all the malfatti have been formed, gently shake the baking sheets and roll the malfatti around in the flour so that all sides are coated. Make sure that the malfatti don't touch or they will stick together. Refrigerate on the baking sheets, uncovered, for 1 hour.

(To store overnight, cover with parchment paper—do not cover with plastic wrap, as this will cause the malfatti to become soggy. Do not freeze malfatti.)

Bring another large pot filled with generously salted water to a simmer over medium-high heat. Add the mafatti and simmer until they float to the surface, 1 to 3 minutes. Remove immediately with a slotted spoon and finish with the brown butter. Serve right away.

CLASSIC GNUDI

SERVES 4

These classic white gnudi are naked, meaning no pasta surrounds the tender ricotta dumpling. They also do not have any greens added to the dough. This is a simple recipe to make and is delicious with many sauces. The gnudi are very delicate, even after cooking, so they are sauced in the serving bowl, not tossed in sauce in a sauté pan as most dumplings are.

400 G/1⅔ CUPS WHOLE-MILK RICOTTA CHEESE, HOMEMADE (SEE PAGE 190) OR STORE-BOUGHT

2 EGGS

50 G/½ CUP + 1 TBSP FINELY GRATED PARMIGIANO-REGGIANO CHEESE

FRESHLY GRATED NUTMEG

85 G/½ CUP + 2 TBSP ALL-PURPOSE FLOUR

1 KG/6 CUPS SEMOLINA FLOUR

SAUCE OF YOUR CHOICE (SUGGESTIONS FOLLOW)

In a medium bowl, combine the ricotta cheese, eggs, and Parmigiano-Reggiano cheese. Season lightly with a few swipes of nutmeg. Add the all-purpose flour and stir with a wooden spoon just until combined.

Line a baking sheet with parchment paper, place 500 g/3 cups of the semolina flour on top, and spread in an even layer. Using two soupspoons or an ice-cream scoop, scoop up about 2 Tbsp of dough and gently drop the dough balls onto the semolina. Make sure the gnudi don't touch or they will stick together. Cover the gnudi with the remaining 500 g/ 3 cups of semolina, distributing it evenly over the top. Refrigerate on the baking sheet, covered with plastic wrap, for at least 8 hours or up to overnight; about halfway through the chilling time, flip each gnudi with a rubber spatula or bench scraper.

Bring a large pot filled with generously salted water to a simmer over medium-high heat. Add the gnudi and simmer until they float to the surface, 1 to 3 minutes. Remove immediately with a slotted spoon to serving bowls; handle the gnudi gently, as they are very delicate, and top with your choice of sauce. Serve right away.

SAUCE PAIRINGS: *Traditionally, gnudi are paired with Pesto (page 172), Tomato Sauce (page 175), or Brown Butter with Sage (page 178). Rabbit Ragù (page 182) or Beef Ragù (page 186) pairs beautifully, as well.*

ZUCCHINI GNUDI

SERVES 4

Zucchini gnudi typify summer. After all, sweet summer squash and fragrant herbs taste of the garden. These dumplings are tender and light, so make sure to keep your water at a gentle simmer, as boiling too vigorously will break them apart. Homemade ricotta cheese transforms these dumplings into something very special: rich, silky, and creamy, with a very elegant feel. If you have some squash blossoms, slice them thinly and use to replace some of the weight of the zucchini in the recipe. Or wilt sliced blossoms gently in butter and use as a sauce for the gnudi.

600 G/21 OZ ZUCCHINI, GRATED ON THE FINEST HOLES OF A BOX GRATER

60 G/6 TBSP KOSHER SALT

2 EGGS, PLUS 2 EGG YOLKS

120 G/½ CUP WHOLE-MILK RICOTTA CHEESE, HOMEMADE (SEE PAGE 190) OR STORE-BOUGHT

100 G/1 CUP + 1 TBSP FINELY GRATED PARMIGIANO-REGGIANO CHEESE

1 TBSP FINELY CHOPPED FRESH MARJORAM

GRATED FRESH ZEST OF ⅔ LEMON

140 G/1 CUP ALL-PURPOSE FLOUR, PLUS MORE AS NEEDED

SAUCE OF YOUR CHOICE (SUGGESTIONS FOLLOW)

In a large bowl, toss the zucchini with 50 g/5 Tbsp of the salt and let sit until the moisture exudes from the zucchini, about 30 minutes. Rinse thoroughly and drain in a colander. Place the zucchini in a kitchen towel and wring until very dry; make sure there is no excess moisture.

In a medium bowl, combine the eggs, egg yolks, ricotta cheese, Parmigiano-Reggiano cheese, marjoram, lemon zest, and remaining 1 Tbsp salt. Add the zucchini and stir with a wooden spoon to combine. Add the flour and mix just until combined. Do not overmix, as this will make the gnudi tough.

Bring a large pot filled with generously salted water to a simmer over medium-high heat. Test the dough by dropping 1 Tbsp of it into the simmering water and cooking for 2 to 3 minutes. If the gnudi does not hold its shape, add a bit more flour to the dough, 1 tsp at a time, and test again. This is a delicate dumpling; add only as much flour as needed to get the gnudi to maintain its shape.

Add the dough, 1 Tbsp at a time, to the simmering water and cook until the dumplings float to the surface, 1 to 3 minutes. Remove immediately with a slotted spoon and finish with your choice of sauce. Serve right away.

SAUCE PAIRINGS: *Serve these gnudi with Tomato Sauce (page 175) or, simply, with melted butter.*

BAKED GNUDI

SERVES 4

Francesco, a wine maker from Florence, visited my restaurant, Lincoln. When I told him about my Italian dumpling research and this book, he told me about the baked gnudi that his mother makes; they are a version of what Florentines sometimes call strozzapreti *(see page 74). Baked gnudi is thought to have resulted from a cook's unsuccessful attempt at making simmered gnudi. An overly loose, soft dough simply disintegrated when dropped into simmering water; the fix was to bake the dough with tomato sauce, meat ragù, or* besciamela *(white sauce). Brilliant! This dish is creamy and rich from the ricotta cheese—think lasagna sans noodles.*

140 G/5 OZ FRESH SPINACH, STEMMED

480 G/2 CUPS WHOLE-MILK RICOTTA CHEESE, HOMEMADE (SEE PAGE 190) OR STORE-BOUGHT

75 G/¾ CUP GRATED PARMIGIANO-REGGIANO CHEESE

2 TBSP ALL-PURPOSE FLOUR, PLUS MORE AS NEEDED

1 EGG

1 TSP KOSHER SALT

FRESHLY GRATED NUTMEG

1½ CUPS (360 ML) TOMATO SAUCE (PAGE 175)

Preheat the oven to 425°F (220°C). Prepare an ice bath by filling a large bowl with ice and cold water. Bring a large pot filled with generously salted water to a boil over medium-high heat. Add the spinach and blanch until wilted, about 2 minutes. Remove immediately from the pot with tongs and transfer to the ice bath. When cool, drain the spinach in a colander. Place the spinach in a kitchen towel and wring until mostly dry; a bit of residual moisture is fine. Finely chop the spinach.

In a medium bowl, combine the spinach, ricotta cheese, 50 g/½ cup of the Parmigiano-Reggiano cheese, the flour, egg, salt, and a few swipes of nutmeg. Stir with a wooden spoon until well combined; the mixture should have the consistency of thick cake batter. Add more flour, 1 Tbsp at a time, until the mixture achieves the proper consistency.

Spread one-half of the tomato sauce in the bottom of a 9-by-13-in (23-by-33-cm) baking dish. Using an ice-cream scoop or two spoons, drop balls of batter, each about the size of a large walnut, into the baking dish, leaving about ½ in (4 cm) between the gnudi (they will spread slightly during baking). Top with the remaining tomato sauce and sprinkle with the remaining 25 g/¼ cup Parmigiano-Reggiano. Bake until the sauce is bubbling and the cheese is beginning to brown, 12 to 15 minutes. Serve right away.

DONZELLINE

This Tuscan dumpling dish is served with salumi (Italian cured meats) in a way very similar to the gnocco fritto of Emilia-Romagna (see page 115). The dough is soft, due to the addition of milk and butter, and the dumpling is lightly crisp and puffy when fried. I will admit that this fritter may not really be traditionally considered a dumpling, but it is comparable to gnocco fritto, and several regions have similar dishes. Since most gnocchi or dumplings are cooked by simmering in water or a soup broth, I think of frying in oil as an alternative cooking method.

220 G/1½ CUPS + 1 TBSP ALL-PURPOSE FLOUR, PLUS MORE FOR DUSTING

KOSHER SALT

2 TBSP UNSALTED BUTTER, AT ROOM TEMPERATURE

65 G/¼ CUP WHOLE MILK, PLUS MORE AS NEEDED

4½ CUPS (900 G) LARD

ABOUT 1 LB (455 G) SLICED SALUMI FOR SERVING

In a medium bowl, combine the flour and ½ tsp salt. Add the butter and, using your fingers, work it into the flour until the mixture is the size of small peas. Add the milk and stir with a wooden spoon until a soft, cohesive dough forms. If the dough is dry or breaks apart, add more milk, 1 Tbsp at a time, until it is soft but not sticky. The dough should be cohesive but not shaggy. Transfer to a floured work surface and knead with your hands several times, until the dough is smooth. Cover the dough with plastic wrap and let rest at room temperature for 30 minutes.

In a medium pot over medium-high heat, heat the lard until it reaches 350°F (180°C) on an instant-read thermometer. Meanwhile, after the dough has rested, roll it on an unfloured surface with a rolling pin until it is about ⅛ in (4 mm) thick. With a knife, cut it into 2-in (5-cm) diamonds.

When the lard is hot, add the dough in batches and fry, turning once with tongs or a metal spatula, until lightly browned, about 4 minutes. Remove from the pot to a platter lined with paper towels and season with salt. Serve warm or at room temperature along with salumi.

GNOCCHI WITH EGG AND RICOTTA

SERVES 4

These simple gnocchi are tender and rich. Your stance on the great Italian debate about egg or no egg in potato gnocchi is up to you (an egg makes the dough more stable and also increases the chance of a weightier mouthfeel but isn't always considered classic). I love these simple dumplings. The dough holds together beautifully and the cheese adds softness to the texture and an added savory flavor. These gnocchi pair well with many sauces, making them very versatile.

430 G/15 OZ RUSSET OR YUKON GOLD POTATOES
110 G/¾ CUP + 1 TBSP ALL-PURPOSE FLOUR, PLUS MORE AS NEEDED AND FOR DUSTING
1 EGG
3½ TBSP WHOLE-MILK RICOTTA CHEESE, HOMEMADE (SEE PAGE 190) OR STORE-BOUGHT
1 TSP KOSHER SALT
SAUCE OF YOUR CHOICE (SUGGESTIONS FOLLOW)

In a medium pot, cover the potatoes with cold water. Bring the water to a simmer over medium-high heat and cook until the potatoes can be easily pierced with a skewer, 15 to 20 minutes. Drain the potatoes in a colander and set aside to cool.

When cool enough to handle, peel the potatoes and rice them into a large bowl. Add the flour, egg, ricotta cheese, and salt and knead with your hands until the dough comes together. The dough should be soft but not sticky. Add more flour, 1 Tbsp at a time, as needed, to achieve this texture.

Sprinkle a small amount of flour on a work surface, scrape the dough onto the surface, and top with another sprinkling of flour. This will help prevent the dough from being too sticky to roll.

Line a baking sheet with parchment paper and dust with flour. Cut off a chunk of dough about the width of two fingers and cover the rest with plastic wrap. On the lightly floured work surface, use your hands to roll the chunk into a log about ½ in (12 mm) in diameter. Do not incorporate too much more flour into the dough, adding just enough so the dough does not stick to the surface. Cut the log into ½- to 1-in (12-mm to 2.5-cm) pieces. Put the gnocchi on the prepared baking sheet and shape the remaining dough. Make sure that the gnocchi don't touch or they will stick together.

(To store, refrigerate on the baking sheet, covered with plastic wrap, for up to 2 days, or freeze on the baking sheet and transfer to an airtight container. Use within 1 month. Do not thaw before cooking.)

Bring a large pot filled with generously salted water to a simmer over medium-high heat. Add the gnocchi and simmer until they float to the surface, 1 to 3 minutes. Remove immediately with a slotted spoon and finish with your choice of sauce. Serve right away.

SAUCE PAIRINGS: *Traditionally, these gnocchi are paired with Pesto (page 172); Tomato Sauce (page 175); Guanciale, Tomato, and Red Onion Sauce (page 176); Brown Butter with Sage (page 178); Fonduta (page 179); Gorgonzola Cream Sauce (page 180); Liver, Pancetta, and Porcini Ragù (page 181); Rabbit Ragù (page 182); Lamb Ragù (page 184); or Beef Ragù (page 186).*

For a traditional Venetian dish, serve these gnocchi as Gnocchi Vicenza (page 147).

POTATO GNOCCHI WITH PARMIGIANO-REGGIANO

SERVES 6 TO 8

After tasting balsamic vinegar at La Vecchia Dispensa in Castelvetro di Modena, I had lunch at Hostaria del Rio, a small restaurant run by three sisters: Luisa, Tiziana, and Laura. Tiziana runs the dining room and Luisa cooks with Laura, the chef. Of course there was gnocchi on the menu and of course I ordered it. The gnocchi was in the style of Emilia-Romagna, with Parmigiano-Reggiano cheese in the dough, a simple sauce of butter or fonduta with Parmigiano-Reggiano, and a good aged balsamic vinegar lightly drizzled over the top. The gnocchi were tender and lovely and I asked the sisters if they would teach me how to make them.

The sisters had something to do that afternoon, so they offered to teach me the following day, Sunday, a day they were closed. I arrived at 10 A.M. for my lesson and, although the restaurant was not open, the three sisters were there and taught me to make these special and delicate gnocchi. Their version does not have salt in the dough, but I have added a little to this recipe. Laura uses the back of a nutmeg grater to make ridges in her gnocchi, but you could use a gnocchi board or fork tines instead. After they taught me how to make this gnocchi, they asked if I wanted to learn anything else. I asked if I could move in for six months.

800 G/28 OZ RUSSET OR YUKON GOLD POTATOES
320 G/2¼ CUPS ALL-PURPOSE FLOUR, PLUS MORE FOR DUSTING
80 G/SCANT 1 CUP FINELY GRATED PARMIGIANO-REGGIANO CHEESE
2 TSP KOSHER SALT
SAUCE OF YOUR CHOICE (SUGGESTIONS FOLLOW)

In a medium pot, cover the potatoes with cold water. Bring the water to a simmer over medium-high heat and cook until the potatoes can be easily pierced with a skewer, 15 to 20 minutes. Drain the potatoes in a colander and set aside to cool.

When cool enough to handle, peel the potatoes and rice them into a large bowl. Add the flour, Parmigiano-Reggiano cheese, and salt and mix by hand until the dough comes together. Transfer to a work surface and knead with your hands several times,

until the dough is smooth and soft. Cover the dough with plastic wrap and let rest at room temperature for 10 minutes.

Line two baking sheets with parchment paper and dust with flour. Cut off a chunk of dough about the width of two fingers and cover the rest with plastic wrap. On a lightly floured work surface, use your hands to roll the chunk into a log about ½ in (12 mm) in diameter. Do not incorporate too much more flour into the dough, adding just enough so that the dough does not stick to the surface. Cut the log into ½- to 1-in (12-mm to 2.5-cm) pieces. With the side of your thumb, gently push each piece against a gnocchi board or the back of the tines of a fork, rolling and flicking the dough to make a curled shape with an indentation on one side and a ridged surface on the other. Put the gnocchi on the prepared baking sheets and shape the remaining dough. Make sure that the gnocchi don't touch or they will stick together.

(To store, refrigerate on the baking sheets, covered with plastic wrap, for up to 2 days, or freeze on the baking sheets and transfer to an airtight container. Use within 1 month. Do not thaw before cooking.)

Bring a large pot filled with generously salted water to a simmer over medium-high heat. Add the gnocchi and simmer until they float to the surface, 1 to 3 minutes. Remove immediately with a slotted spoon and finish with your choice of sauce. Serve right away.

SAUCE PAIRINGS: *Traditionally, gnocchi with Parmigiano-Reggiano are paired with Tomato Sauce (page 175); Brown Butter with Sage (page 178); Fonduta (page 179); Gorgonzola Cream Sauce (page 180); Liver, Pancetta, and Porcini Ragù (page 181); Rabbit Ragù (page 182); or Beef Ragù (page 186).*

LA STOPPA'S
CHICCHE DELLA NONNA

SERVES 5

Carla at La Stoppa winery outside of Piacenza taught me this recipe. The method was unique compared to other chicche recipes I knew. She puréed the cooked spinach into a thick paste, rather than finely chopping it. The dough is elegant and soft, without any strands of spinach. The texture of the dumplings is tender and almost ethereal. We ate this gnocchi with a creamy tomato sauce and a cream-based Gorgonzola sauce, both incredible. Carla also likes to make this recipe with winter squash purée in place of spinach purée.

255 G/9 OZ FRESH SPINACH, STEMMED

570 G/20 OZ RUSSET OR YUKON GOLD POTATOES

2 TBSP EXTRA-VIRGIN OLIVE OIL

1 EGG YOLK

30 G/⅓ CUP FINELY GRATED PARMIGIANO-REGGIANO CHEESE

230 G/1½ CUPS + 3 TBSP ALL-PURPOSE FLOUR, PLUS MORE FOR DUSTING

2 TBSP WHOLE-MILK RICOTTA CHEESE, HOMEMADE (SEE PAGE 190) OR STORE-BOUGHT

2 TSP KOSHER SALT

½ NUTMEG, FRESHLY GRATED

SAUCE OF YOUR CHOICE (SUGGESTIONS FOLLOW)

Prepare an ice bath by filling a large bowl with ice and cold water. Bring a large pot filled with generously salted water to a boil over medium-high heat. Add the spinach and blanch until wilted, about 2 minutes. Remove immediately from the pot with tongs and transfer to the ice bath. When cool, drain the spinach in a colander. Place the spinach in a kitchen towel and wring until mostly dry; a bit of residual moisture is fine.

In a medium pot, cover the potatoes with cold water. Bring the water to a simmer over medium-high heat and cook until the potatoes can be easily pierced with a skewer,

15 to 20 minutes. Drain the potatoes in a colander and set aside to cool.

In a blender or food processor, process the spinach, olive oil, and egg yolk until they form a thick, smooth paste.

When the potatoes are cool enough to handle, peel them and rice them into a large bowl. Add the spinach mixture, the Parmigiano-Reggiano cheese, flour, ricotta cheese, salt, and nutmeg and mix with your hands until the dough comes together. Transfer to a work surface and knead with your hands a few times, until the dough is smooth and soft.

Line a baking sheet with parchment paper and dust with flour. Cut off a chunk of dough about the width of two fingers and cover the rest with plastic wrap. On a lightly floured work surface, roll the chunk into a log about ½ in (12 mm) in diameter. Do not incorporate too much more flour into the dough, adding just enough so that the dough does not stick to the surface. Cut the log into ½- to 1-in (12-mm to 2.5-cm) pieces. Put the chicche on the prepared baking sheet and shape the remaining dough. Make sure that the chicche don't touch or they will stick together.

(To store, refrigerate on the baking sheet, covered with plastic wrap, for up to 2 days, or freeze on the baking sheet and transfer to an airtight container. Use within 1 month. Do not thaw before cooking.)

Bring another large pot filled with generously salted water to a simmer over medium-high heat. Add the chicche and simmer until they float to the surface, 1 to 3 minutes. Remove immediately with a slotted spoon and finish with your choice of sauce. Serve right away.

SAUCE PAIRINGS: *Traditionally, chicche is paired with Tomato Sauce (page 175) or Gorgonzola Cream Sauce (page 180).*

CHICCHE VERDI DEL NONNO

SERVES 4 TO 6

This recipe for gnocchi with brown butter and sage is an adaptation of one that was featured in Saveur magazine in October 2009. The story goes that Giuseppe Verdi, whose parents owned an osteria in the city of Parma, was as much a cook and gardener as he was a great composer. This was a dish that his mother would make. It is a unique gnocchi, as it is sautéed and crispy on the exterior yet tender inside. These gnocchi are served with a drizzle of brown butter, rather than a moister sauce, and have a nutty sweetness.

GNOCCHI

455 G/1 LB RUSSET OR YUKON GOLD POTATOES

115 G/¼ LB FRESH SPINACH, STEMMED

215 G/1¼ CUPS SEMOLINA FLOUR, PLUS MORE FOR DUSTING

2 EGGS, BEATEN

2 TSP KOSHER SALT

18 TBSP (255 G) UNSALTED BUTTER

16 FRESH SAGE LEAVES, MINCED

FRESHLY GRATED NUTMEG

KOSHER SALT AND FRESHLY GROUND BLACK PEPPER

¼ CUP (60 ML) EXTRA-VIRGIN OLIVE OIL

3 TBSP FINELY GRATED PARMIGIANO-REGGIANO CHEESE

Make the gnocchi: In a medium pot, cover the potatoes with cold water. Bring the water to a simmer over medium-high heat and cook until the potatoes can be easily pierced with a skewer, 15 to 20 minutes. Drain the potatoes in a colander and set aside to cool.

When cool enough to handle, peel the potatoes and rice them into a large bowl.

Heat a 12-in (30.5-cm) skillet over medium-high heat. Add the spinach and 1 Tbsp water and cook until the spinach is wilted, about 30 seconds. Drain immediately in a colander. Place the spinach in a kitchen towel and wring until mostly dry; a bit of residual moisture is fine. Finely chop the spinach.

Add the chopped spinach and semolina flour to the potatoes in the bowl and stir with a wooden spoon until combined. Form a well in the center of the mixture and add the eggs and salt to the well. Using a fork, mix the eggs into the potato mixture until the ingredients are well blended.

CONTINUED

Transfer the dough to a work surface lightly dusted with semolina and knead with your hands until the dough is moist and soft.

Line two baking sheets with parchment paper and dust with semolina. Cut off a chunk of dough about the width of two fingers and cover the rest with plastic wrap. On an unfloured work surface, roll the chunk into a log about ½ in (12 mm) in diameter. Cut the log into ½- to 1-in (12-mm to 2.5-cm) pieces. Put the gnocchi on the prepared baking sheets and shape the remaining dough. Make sure that the gnocchi don't touch or they will stick together.

Melt 10 Tbsp (140 g) of the butter in a 10-in (25-cm) skillet over medium heat; cook, swirling, until the butter browns, about 6 minutes. Add the sage and a few swipes of nutmeg; season with salt and pepper. Remove from the heat; set aside.

Work in four batches to sauté the gnocchi, wiping the skillet clean between batches. For each batch, add 2 Tbsp butter and 1 Tbsp olive oil to a 12-in (30.5-cm) skillet over medium-high heat. Add one-quarter of the gnocchi and cook, flipping once, until golden brown, 3 to 4 minutes. Transfer to a baking sheet. After the final batch of gnocchi has been sautéed, return all of them to the skillet. Pour the brown butter sauce over the gnocchi and toss over medium-high heat just until hot. Remove immediately with a slotted spoon to a serving platter and top with grated Parmigiano-Reggiano cheese. Serve right away.

PISAREI E FASO

SERVES 8

Literally translated as "babies' penises," pisarei are always served in soup. Pisarei e faso, the soup that features pisarei, is typical of Piacenza in Emilia-Romagna, the region known for rich pasta sauces and wonderful salumi and cheeses. This is a peasant dish, made from inexpensive ingredients and fortified with lardo—cured pork fatback—for flavor. Typically, this soup has a soft red color; it uses less tomato than other dumpling-based soups with a more pronounced tomato presence. This soup is hearty, rich, and filling.

DUMPLINGS

230 G/1 CUP WATER, PLUS MORE AS NEEDED

250 G/2 CUPS DRIED BREAD CRUMBS

500 G/3½ CUPS + 1 TBSP ALL-PURPOSE FLOUR, PLUS MORE FOR DUSTING

2 TSP KOSHER SALT

SOUP

¼ CUP (60 ML) EXTRA-VIRGIN OLIVE OIL

2 BAY LEAVES

LEAVES FROM ONE 4-IN (10-CM) SPRIG ROSEMARY

1 MEDIUM YELLOW ONION, CUT INTO SMALL DICE

3 CARROTS, MINCED

9 OZ (255 G) LARDO OR PANCETTA, CUT INTO SMALL DICE

1 CUP (240 ML) RED WINE

2 CUPS (400 G) CANNED WHOLE PEELED TOMATOES, PURÉED AND STRAINED

4 QT (3.8 L) BEEF OR VEGETABLE STOCK

2 TBSP FINELY CHOPPED FRESH ITALIAN PARSLEY

2½ CUPS (500 G) DRIED BORLOTTI BEANS, SOAKED OVERNIGHT IN WATER TO COVER, DRAINED

¾ CUP (170 G) UNSALTED BUTTER, CUT INTO ¼-IN (6-MM) PATS

1 CUP (90 G) FINELY GRATED PARMIGIANO-REGGIANO CHEESE, PLUS MORE FOR SERVING

CONTINUED

Make the dumplings: Bring the water to a boil over high heat. In the bowl of a food processor, process the bread crumbs until finely ground.

In a large bowl, mix the bread crumbs, flour, and salt. Add the boiling water and mix with a wooden spoon, adding more water, 1 Tbsp at a time, until the dough is soft but not sticky. Transfer to an unfloured work surface and knead a few times, until the dough is a cohesive ball. This dough doesn't need to rest.

Line two baking sheets with parchment paper and dust with flour. Cut off a chunk of dough about the width of two fingers and cover the rest with plastic wrap. On an unfloured work surface, use your hands to roll the chunk into a log about ½ in (12 mm) in diameter. Break off small knobs of dough, each one about the size of a peanut. Working with one piece at a time, with the side of your thumb, gently press down on the dough while rolling along the work surface and flicking up. This will create a small gnocchi without ridges. Put the pisarei on the prepared baking sheets and shape the remaining dough. Make sure that the pisarei don't touch or they will stick together.

(To store, refrigerate on the baking sheets, covered with plastic wrap, for up to 2 days, or freeze on the baking sheets and transfer to an airtight container. Use within 1 month. Do not thaw before cooking.)

Make the soup: In a large pot, warm the olive oil over medium heat. Add the bay leaves, rosemary, onion, carrots, and lardo and cook until the vegetables are tender but not browned, 3 to 5 minutes. Add the wine, raise the heat to medium-high, and cook until the wine reduces by half, 2 to 3 minutes. Add the tomatoes, beef stock, parsley, and beans and turn the heat to medium. Cook at a gentle simmer until the beans are tender, 20 to 30 minutes.

When the beans are tender, raise the heat to medium-high. Add the pisarei, butter, and Parmigiano-Reggiano cheese. Cook until the pisarei are cooked through, about 5 minutes. The broth should be thick with vegetables, beans, and lardo. Remove the bay leaves.

Ladle the soup into individual bowls and top with grated Parmigiano-Reggiano. Serve right away.

PASSATELLI

SERVES 4

Passatelli are rustic dumplings made from a dense dough that is extruded through a passatelli maker or the large holes of a potato ricer. They can be found on dinner tables across Emilia-Romagna and the Marche, and are most often served in a light chicken broth, though they can also be dressed with sauce. Similar to the debate about egg or no egg in potato gnocchi, the passatelli debate is about whether or not to add flour to the dough. Passatelli are not a garnish for a broth, but rather the main component of the dish.

250 G/2 CUPS DRIED BREAD CRUMBS

150 G/1½ CUPS + 2 TBSP FINELY GRATED PARMIGIANO-REGGIANO CHEESE, PLUS MORE FOR SERVING

2 TBSP EXTRA-VIRGIN OLIVE OIL

KOSHER SALT

GRATED ZEST OF ½ LEMON

½ SMALL NUTMEG, FRESHLY GRATED

4 EGGS, LIGHTLY BEATEN, PLUS 1 EGG WHITE

3 CUPS (720 ML) CHICKEN STOCK (PAGE 189)

In the bowl of a food processor, process the bread crumbs until finely ground.

In a large bowl, combine the bread crumbs, Parmigiano-Reggiano cheese, olive oil, ¼ tsp salt, lemon zest, and nutmeg. Make a well in the center of the bread crumb mixture and add the eggs and egg white. Mix with your hands until a cohesive dough is formed, 3 to 5 minutes; the dough should be soft, moist, and hold together in a ball. (If the dough is dry or breaks apart, add water, 1 tsp at a time, until the dough achieves the proper consistency.) Cover the dough with plastic wrap and let rest at room temperature for 1 hour.

In a large pot, bring the chicken stock to a gentle simmer over medium-high heat, just until it's warm. Taste and season with salt.

If the dough no longer feels soft and moist, mix in more water, 1 tsp at a time, to restore its consistency.

Line a baking sheet with parchment paper. Cut the dough into four pieces. Over the prepared baking sheet, press a piece of dough through a passatelli maker or a potato ricer with large holes. The strands of passatelli will vary in length as they are extruded. Repeat with the remaining dough.

Bring another large pot filled with generously salted water to a simmer. Add the passatelli and simmer until they float to the surface, about 1 minute. Remove immediately with a slotted spoon and divide among four bowls. Ladle the warm stock over the passatelli and serve with grated Parmigiano-Reggiano.

ROYALE BOLOGNESE

SERVES 4

I was visiting Bologna and had read about royale bolognese, a firm Parmigiano-Reggiano dumpling served in a flavorful broth, but had never seen it on a menu nor heard anyone speak of it in the States. I had a conversation with Luisa, my mentor in Bologna, about a family meal she had cooked the previous week. She mentioned royale bolognese, and I was thrilled to learn the dish from her. Luisa says you should not overcook the royale—around three hours of cooking seems to be just right. The broth is flavored by the Parmigiano-scented royale while it simmers. One of my cooks said the soup is one of the best things he has ever eaten. I agree.

ROYALE
2 EGGS
60 G/¼ CUP UNSALTED BUTTER, AT ROOM TEMPERATURE
60 G/⅔ CUP FINELY GRATED PARMIGIANO-REGGIANO CHEESE
120 G/¾ CUP + 1 TBSP ALL-PURPOSE FLOUR
1 TSP KOSHER SALT
FRESHLY GRATED NUTMEG

BROTH
½ CHICKEN, CUT INTO 4 PIECES
½ LB (230 G) BEEF STEW MEAT
¼ LB (115 G) PARMIGIANO-REGGIANO CHEESE RINDS
1 CARROT, CUT INTO 1-IN (2.5-CM) CHUNKS
2 STALKS CELERY, CUT INTO 1-IN (2.5-CM) CHUNKS
1 YELLOW ONION, CUT INTO 1-IN (2.5-CM) CHUNKS
5 WHOLE CLOVES
KOSHER SALT
FRESHLY GRATED NUTMEG

Make the royale: In a medium bowl, combine the eggs, butter, Parmigiano-Reggiano cheese, flour, salt, and a few swipes of nutmeg and knead with your hands until the dough comes together. On an unfloured work surface, roll the dough to form a ball, then roll it roughly into a sausage shape, about 2 in (5 cm) in diameter. Wrap in cheesecloth and tie with butcher's twine.

Make the broth: In a medium pot, combine the chicken, beef, Parmigiano-Reggiano cheese rinds, carrot, celery, onion, and cloves. Add just enough water to cover and bring to a simmer over medium-high heat. Add the wrapped royale and gently simmer for 3 hours. Using tongs, transfer the royale to a baking sheet. Set a second baking sheet on top and place two large cans (such as cans of tomatoes) on top. Let cool to room temperature, about 1 hour, then refrigerate with the weights until cold, at least 4 hours or up to overnight.

Set a fine-mesh sieve over a large bowl. Strain the broth into the bowl and discard the solid pieces. Cover and refrigerate the broth.

When you are ready to serve, in a large saucepan, bring the broth to a simmer over medium-low heat. Remove the cheesecloth from around the royale and cut the royale into ½-in (12-mm) cubes. Add the cubes to the broth and cook until heated through, 5 to 7 minutes. Season with salt and a few swipes of nutmeg. Serve right away.

PARMIGIANO-REGGIANO CHEESE RINDS

This recipe calls for rinds of Parmigiano-Reggiano. These rinds are, in fact, just cheese that has become oxidized from exposure to the air. They are full of flavor, and most Italian cooks save them up to add richness and complexity to stock for soups and risotto.

CRESCENTINA

SERVES 4 TO 6

These fried "gnocchi" aren't poached dumplings, but the Italians call them gnocchi *nevertheless. Featured in the cuisine of Emilia-Romagna, where the dish is known as* gnocco fritto, *it is an accompaniment to various salumi and is served as an appetizer or an entrée. The dough can be made with water for a crisper gnocco, or with milk for a softer texture. Recipes will often use yeast or baking soda as the leavener. I prefer yeast, because it doesn't have the tinny flavor that baking soda can impart. You can use vegetable oil for frying instead of lard, if you like.*

2 TSP ACTIVE DRY YEAST

120 G/½ CUP WHOLE MILK, WARM

270 G/1¾ CUPS + 3 TBSP ALL-PURPOSE FLOUR, PLUS MORE FOR DUSTING

KOSHER SALT

4 TSP LARD, PLUS 4½ CUPS (900 G)

ABOUT 1 LB (455 G) SLICED SALUMI FOR SERVING

In a small bowl, stir together the yeast and warm milk until dissolved. Set aside until the yeast blooms and becomes foamy, about 10 minutes.

In a medium bowl, combine the flour and ½ tsp salt. Add the 4 tsp lard and, using your fingers, work it into the flour until the lard lumps are the size of small peas. Stir in the yeast-milk mixture, 1 Tbsp at a time, until the dough is soft but not sticky. (If the dough is still too dry, add warm water, 1 Tbsp at a time, until the correct consistency is reached.) Transfer to a floured work surface and knead with your hands several times, until the dough is smooth. Lightly oil a bowl with lard and invert it over the dough. Let the dough rise at room temperature until doubled in size, about 1 hour.

In a medium pot, add the remaining 4½ cups (900 g) lard and heat over medium heat until it reaches 350°F (180°C) on an instant-read thermometer. Meanwhile, when the dough has risen, roll it with a rolling pin on a floured work surface until it is about ⅜ in (1 cm) thick. With a knife, cut the dough into 2-in (5-cm) diamonds.

When the lard is hot, add the dough and fry, turning once with tongs or a metal spatula, until lightly golden, about 4 minutes. Remove from the lard to a plate lined with paper towels and season with salt. Serve warm or at room temperature along with salumi.

MENIETTI IN VEGETABLE SOUP

SERVES 6

These simple, tender dumplings from Liguria are easy to make and very flavorful when simmered in broth. I think what I love most about them is the way the flavor of olive oil perfumes the dumplings and complements a simple vegetable soup.

MENIETTI

400 G/2¾ CUPS + 2 TBSP ALL-PURPOSE FLOUR

100 G/⅓ CUP + 1½ TBSP WHOLE MILK

50 G/¼ CUP EXTRA-VIRGIN OLIVE OIL

SEMOLINA FLOUR FOR DUSTING

SOUP

½ CUP (120 ML) EXTRA-VIRGIN OLIVE OIL

2 LARGE LEEKS, WHITE PARTS ONLY, THINLY SLICED INTO HALF MOONS

2 CARROTS, CHOPPED INTO SMALL DICE

2 STALKS CELERY, CHOPPED INTO SMALL DICE

LEAVES FROM 1 SPRIG FRESH ROSEMARY

2 BAY LEAVES

8 CUPS (2 L) CHICKEN STOCK (PAGE 189)

2 TBSP + 1 TSP KOSHER SALT

PARMIGIANO-REGGIANO CHEESE FOR GRATING

Make the menietti: Place the all-purpose flour in a large bowl. Add the milk and olive oil and, using a fork, stir the liquid into the flour until it is absorbed and small lumps form.

Line two baking sheets with parchment paper and dust with semolina flour.

Fill a small bowl with water and lightly dampen your hands with the water. Take about 1 Tbsp of the lumpy flour mixture and roll it between your moistened hands to form a ball. Then roll the ball between your palms to make a cigarette-shaped dumpling about ⅛ in (3 mm) thick and 2 in (5 cm) long. All the menietti will look a little different, and a little shagginess in the dough is okay; the menietti do not need to be perfectly consistent in size. Put the menietti on the prepared baking sheets and shape the remaining dough. Make sure that the menietti don't touch or they will stick together.

Make the soup: In a large pot, warm the olive oil over medium-high heat. Add the leeks, carrots, celery, rosemary, and bay leaves and cook, stirring occasionally, until the vegetables are tender, 8 to 10 minutes. If the vegetables begin to brown, lower the heat. Add the chicken stock and salt, raise the heat to medium-high, and simmer until the flavors meld, 10 to 15 minutes.

Add the menietti and cook, adjusting the heat as needed to maintain a simmer. Cook until the menietti are tender, 6 to 8 minutes.

Ladle into six individual bowls and top with grated Parmigiano-Reggiano cheese. Serve right away.

SUGELI WITH POTATOES AND GARLIC

SERVES 6 TO 8

Sugeli are made with a very simple dough and have a shape that resembles orecchiette. Their traditional sauce is a white sauce with brusso, a soft fermented cheese made from the milk of Brigasca sheep. Mendatica, a mountain town in this Maritime Alps region, is the home of cucina bianca, *or "white cooking." Nearly every dish in this region includes dairy and is therefore some shade of white. Sugeli are a signature dish of the Maritime Alps, along with other lightly colored foods, including other dairy products and vegetables such as potatoes, turnips, leeks, and garlic. Despite this region's proximity to the sea,* cucina bianca *is very different from typical Mediterranean cooking.*

SUGELI
500 G/3½ CUPS + 1 TBSP ALL-PURPOSE FLOUR, PLUS MORE FOR DUSTING
50 G/¼ CUP EXTRA-VIRGIN OLIVE OIL
2 TSP KOSHER SALT
240 G/1 CUP + 1 TBSP WATER
SEMOLINA FLOUR FOR DUSTING

POTATOES AND GARLIC
10½ OZ (300 G) NEW POTATOES
¼ CUP (60 ML) EXTRA-VIRGIN OLIVE OIL
4 TBSP (55 G) UNSALTED BUTTER, CUT INTO CUBES
4 GARLIC CLOVES, CUT INTO VERY THIN SLICES
2 TSP KOSHER SALT
¼ CUP + 1 TBSP (70 G) WHOLE-MILK RICOTTA CHEESE, HOMEMADE (SEE PAGE 190) OR STORE-BOUGHT
PARMIGIANO-REGGIANO CHEESE FOR GRATING

Make the sugeli: In a medium bowl, combine the all-purpose flour, olive oil, salt, and water and knead with your hands until a soft dough is formed, 5 to 8 minutes. Cover the dough with plastic wrap and let rest at room temperature for 30 minutes.

Line two baking sheets with parchment paper and dust with semolina flour. Cut off about one-eighth of the dough and leave the rest covered with plastic wrap. On a work surface lightly dusted with all-purpose flour, use your hands to roll the dough into a log about ½ in (12 mm) in diameter. Cut the log into ½-in (12-mm) pieces. Turn each piece cut-side up and, with your thumb, press on the center to make a round dumpling that is thin and flat in the middle and slightly thicker at the edge. Put the sugeli on the prepared baking sheets and shape the remaining dough. Make sure that the sugeli do not touch or they will stick together.

(To store, refrigerate on the baking sheets, covered with plastic wrap, for up to 2 days, or freeze on the baking sheets and transfer to an airtight container. Use within 1 month. Do not thaw before cooking.)

Prepare the potatoes and garlic: In a medium pot, cover the potatoes with cold water. Bring to a simmer over medium-high heat and cook until the potatoes can be easily pierced with a skewer, 15 to 20 minutes. Drain the potatoes in a colander and set aside to cool. When potatoes are cool enough to handle, cut into ¼-in (6-mm) slices. Set aside.

Bring a large pot filled with generously salted water to a simmer over medium-high heat. Add the sugeli and simmer until tender, 2 to 3 minutes. Meanwhile, in a 12-in (30.5-cm) sauté pan, warm the olive oil, butter, and garlic over medium-low heat and cook until the garlic is fragrant and no longer raw, 3 to 4 minutes. If the garlic begins to brown, lower the heat. Add the potatoes and the sugeli, using a slotted spoon to transfer them directly from the cooking water. Stir gently and cook until heated through, about 2 minutes. Add the salt and ricotta cheese and stir gently. Transfer to a serving dish and top with grated Parmigiano-Reggiano cheese. Serve right away.

CHICKPEA GNOCCHETTI

SERVES 4

Chickpea gnocchetti, made with cooked chickpeas, are slightly denser than most dumplings, especially ones that contain ricotta or potato, such as ricotta cavatelli or potato gnocchi. This recipe is my adaptation of one that appeared in the March 2012 issue of the American publication La Cucina Italiana. *You can make these gnocchetti larger, but I think they are wonderful when small.*

140 G/1 CUP COOKED CHICKPEAS

2 EGGS

2 TBSP WARM WATER

200 G/1⅓ CUPS + 1 TBSP ALL-PURPOSE FLOUR, PLUS MORE FOR DUSTING

KOSHER SALT

SAUCE OF YOUR CHOICE (SUGGESTIONS FOLLOW)

In a blender or food processor, combine the chickpeas, eggs, and water. Purée until smooth, then transfer to a large bowl. Add the flour, season with salt, and gently knead with your hands until a soft dough forms, 2 to 3 minutes. This dough doesn't need to rest.

Line a baking sheet with parchment paper and dust with flour. Cut off a chunk of dough about the width of two fingers and cover the rest with plastic wrap. On a lightly floured work surface, use your hands to roll the chunk into a log about ½ in (12 mm) in diameter. Cut the log into ½-in (12-mm) pieces. With the side of your thumb, gently push each piece against a gnocchi board or the back of the tines of a fork, rolling and flicking the dough to make a curled shape with an indentation on one side and a ridged surface on the other. Put the gnocchetti on the prepared baking sheet and shape the remaining dough. Make sure the gnocchetti don't touch or they will stick together.

(To store, refrigerate on the baking sheet, covered with plastic wrap, for up to 2 days, or freeze on the baking sheet and transfer to an airtight container. Use within 1 month. Do not thaw before cooking.)

Bring a large pot filled with generously salted water to a simmer over medium-high heat. Add the gnocchetti and simmer until tender, about 3 minutes. Remove immediately with a slotted spoon and finish with your choice of sauce. Serve right away.

SAUCE PAIRINGS: *Serve these gnocchetti with Pesto (page 172) or Lamb Ragù (page 184).*

TROFIE WITH WHEAT BRAN
SERVES 6

These trofie are tender in texture and rustic in flavor with the rich and earthy flavor of wheat bran. The earthiness pairs well with heartier meat sauces like beef and lamb.

510 G/3½ CUPS + 2 TBSP "00" FLOUR (SEE PAGE 16)
30 G/1 CUP WHEAT BRAN
2 TSP KOSHER SALT
225 G/1 CUP WARM WATER, PLUS MORE AS NEEDED
SEMOLINA FLOUR FOR DUSTING
SAUCE OF YOUR CHOICE (SUGGESTIONS FOLLOW)

In a large bowl or the bowl of a stand mixer fitted with a dough hook attachment, combine the "00" flour, wheat bran, and salt. Mix with your hands or on medium-low speed to combine. Add the water and mix for 1 to 2 minutes. Add more water, 1 Tbsp at a time, until the dough just comes together. If there is any dry flour remaining in the bottom of the bowl, stop mixing and turn the dough over a few times with your hands to get the dry flour to adhere to the wetter dough mass, then continue mixing. Knead for a total of 5 minutes; the dough should be smooth and cohesive. Cover the dough with plastic wrap and let rest at room temperature for 1 hour.

Line two baking sheets with parchment paper and dust with semolina flour. Cut off a chunk of dough about the width of two fingers and cover the rest with plastic wrap. On an unfloured work surface, use your hands to roll the chunk into a log ¼ in (6 mm) in diameter. Cut the log into chickpea-size

pieces. Working with one piece at a time, using your hands, roll the dough back and forth into a rope about ⅛ in (3 mm) thick and 3 in (7.5 cm) long. Then roll the rope toward yourself, applying pressure with a metal bench scraper held at an angle to the rope; this will give the trofie a spiral shape. Put the trofie on the prepared baking sheets and shape the remaining dough. Make sure that the trofie don't touch or they will stick together.

(To store, refrigerate on the baking sheets, covered with plastic wrap, for up to 2 days, or freeze on the baking sheets and transfer to an airtight container. Use within 1 month. Do not thaw before cooking.)

Bring a large pot filled with generously salted water to a simmer over medium-high heat. Add the trofie and simmer until al dente, 1 to 3 minutes. Remove immediately with a slotted spoon and finish with your choice of sauce. Serve right away.

SAUCE PAIRINGS: *Traditionally, trofie are paired with Pesto (page 172), but these wheat bran trofie also go well with Lamb Ragù (page 184) and Beef Ragù (page 186).*

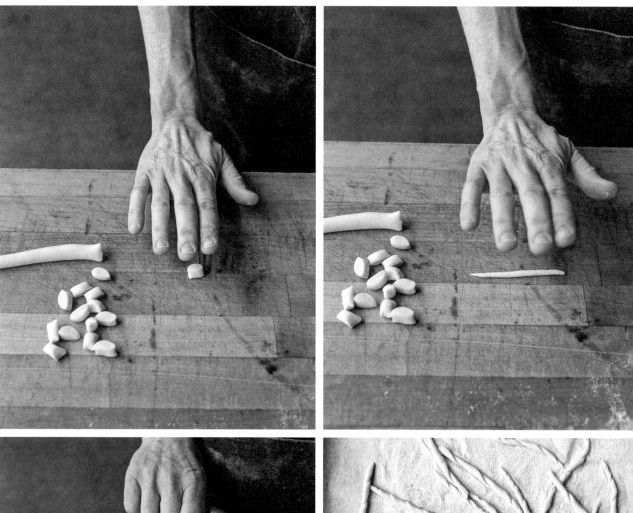

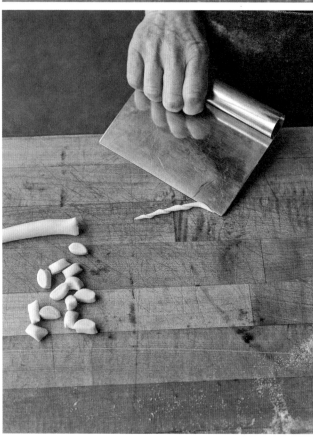

SEMOLINA TROFIE

SERVES 6

This is the toothiest of trofie—yet not so toothy compared to some dumplings—thanks to the semolina flour, which creates a strong and sturdy structure. This slightly chewy dumpling is classically paired with basil pesto, a very traditional sauce from Liguria, the region from which trofie hail.

255 G/1½ CUPS SEMOLINA FLOUR, PLUS MORE FOR DUSTING

255 G/1¾ CUPS + 1 TBSP ALL-PURPOSE FLOUR

2 TSP KOSHER SALT

255 G/1 CUP + 1 TBSP WARM WATER, PLUS MORE AS NEEDED

PESTO (PAGE 172)

In a large bowl or the bowl of a stand mixer fitted with a dough hook attachment, combine the semolina flour, all-purpose flour, and salt. Add the water and stir with a wooden spoon or mix on medium speed until a cohesive but not sticky dough forms, 1 to 2 minutes. Add more water, 1 Tbsp at a time, and knead with your hands or on medium speed until the dough is smooth and soft without being sticky or dry, about 8 minutes more. Cover the dough with plastic wrap and let rest at room temperature for 1 hour.

Line two baking sheets with parchment paper and dust with semolina flour. Cut off a chunk of dough about the width of two fingers and cover the rest with plastic wrap. On an unfloured work surface, use your hands to roll the chunk into a log ¼ in (6 mm) in diameter. Cut the log into chickpea-size pieces. Working with one piece at a time, using your hands, roll the dough back and forth into a rope about ⅛ in (3 mm) thick and 3 in (7.5 cm) long. Then roll the rope toward yourself, applying pressure with a metal bench scraper held at an angle to the rope; this will give the trofie a spiral shape. Put the trofie on the prepared baking sheets and shape the remaining dough. Make sure that the trofie don't touch or they will stick together.

(To store, refrigerate on the baking sheets, covered with plastic wrap, for up to 2 days, or freeze on the baking sheets and transfer to an airtight container. Use within 1 month. Do not thaw before cooking.)

Bring a large pot filled with generously salted water to a simmer over medium-high heat. Add the trofie and simmer until al dente, 1 to 3 minutes. Remove immediately with a slotted spoon and finish with the pesto. Serve right away.

POTATO TROFIE

SERVES 8

All the trofie recipes in this book yield tender dumplings, but this one is the most tender of them all. The addition of potato builds in moisture and softens the texture of the noodle.

400 G/14 OZ RUSSET OR YUKON GOLD POTATOES
570 G/4 CUPS ALL-PURPOSE FLOUR
2 TSP KOSHER SALT
2 EGGS
SEMOLINA FLOUR FOR DUSTING
SAUCE OF YOUR CHOICE (SUGGESTIONS FOLLOW)

In a medium pot, cover the potatoes with cold water. Bring to a simmer over medium-high heat and cook until the potatoes can be easily pierced with a skewer, 15 to 20 minutes. Drain the potatoes in a colander and set aside to cool.

When cool enough to handle, peel the potatoes and rice them into a large bowl or the bowl of a stand mixer fitted with a dough hook attachment. Add the all-purpose flour and salt. Mix with your hands or on medium-low speed until roughly combined, about 1 minute. Add 1 of the eggs and mix for 1 to 2 minutes, then add the remaining egg and mix until the dough just comes together. If there is any dry flour remaining in the bottom of the bowl, stop mixing and turn the dough over a few times with your hands to get the dry flour to adhere to the wetter dough mass, then continue mixing. Knead for a total of 5 minutes; the dough should be

soft and cohesive, but not wet. Cover the dough with plastic wrap and let rest at room temperature for 1 hour.

Line two baking sheets with parchment paper and dust with semolina flour. Cut off a chunk of dough about the width of two fingers and cover the rest with plastic wrap. On an unfloured work surface, use your hands to roll the chunk into a log ¼ in (6 mm) in diameter. Cut the log into chickpea-size pieces. Working with one piece at a time, using your hands, roll the dough back and forth into a rope about ⅛ in (3 mm) thick and 3 in (7.5 cm) long. Then roll the rope toward yourself, applying pressure with a metal bench scraper held at an angle to the rope; this will give the trofie a spiral shape. Put the trofie on the prepared baking sheets and shape the remaining dough. Make sure that the trofie don't touch or they will stick together.

(To store, refrigerate on the baking sheets, covered with plastic wrap, for up to 2 days, or freeze on the baking sheets and transfer to an airtight container. Use within 1 month. Do not thaw before cooking.)

Bring a large pot filled with generously salted water to a simmer over medium-high heat. Add the trofie and simmer until al dente, 1 to 3 minutes. Remove immediately with a slotted spoon and finish with your choice of sauce. Serve right away.

SAUCE PAIRINGS: *Traditionally, these trofie are served with Pesto (page 172); Tomato Sauce (page 175); Liver, Pancetta, and Porcini Ragù (page 181); Rabbit Ragù (page 182); Lamb Ragù (page 184); or Beef Ragù (page 186).*

DONDERETS

SERVES 4

This type of gnocchi comes from Langhe, in Piedmont, and the dough features the richness of egg yolks and cheese. The texture has been refined from the older, traditional recipes, which have a loose batter like spätzli, to a soft dumpling that incorporates potato. It is said to be the cousin of dunderi, a ricotta-based dumpling from Campania, and is not so different from the potato and Parmigiano-Reggiano gnocchi of Emilia-Romagna.

570 G/20 OZ RUSSET OR YUKON GOLD POTATOES

70 G/½ CUP ALL-PURPOSE FLOUR, PLUS MORE FOR DUSTING

2 EGG YOLKS

75 G/⅔ CUP + 1 TBSP FINELY GRATED PARMIGIANO-REGGIANO CHEESE

2 TSP KOSHER SALT

SEMOLINA FLOUR FOR DUSTING

SAUCE OF YOUR CHOICE (SUGGESTIONS FOLLOW)

In a medium pot, cover the potatoes with cold water. Bring to a simmer over medium-high heat and cook until the potatoes can be easily pierced with a skewer, 15 to 20 minutes. Drain the potatoes in a colander and set aside to cool.

When cool enough to handle, peel the potatoes and rice them into a large bowl. Add the all-purpose flour, egg yolks, Parmigiano-Reggiano cheese, and salt and mix with your hands until the dough comes together. Transfer to a work surface and knead with your hands several times, until the dough is cohesive.

Line a baking sheet with parchment paper and dust with semolina flour. Cut off a chunk of dough about the width of two fingers and cover the rest with plastic wrap. On a work surface lightly dusted with all-purpose flour, use your hands to roll the chunk into a log about ½ in (12 mm) in diameter. Do not incorporate too much more flour into the dough; add just enough so that the dough does not stick to the surface. Cut the log into ½- to 1-in (12-mm to 2.5-cm) pieces. With the side of your thumb, gently push each piece against a gnocchi board or the back of the tines of a fork, rolling and flicking the dough to make a curled shape with an indentation on one side and a ridged surface on the other. Put the gnocchi on the prepared baking sheet and shape the remaining dough. Make sure that the gnocchi don't touch or they will stick together.

(To store, refrigerate on the baking sheet, covered with plastic wrap, for up to 2 days, or freeze on the baking sheet and transfer to an airtight container. Use within 1 month. Do not thaw before cooking.)

Bring a large pot filled with generously salted water to a simmer over medium-high heat. Add the gnocchi and simmer until they float to the surface, 1 to 3 minutes. Remove immediately with a slotted spoon and finish with your choice of sauce. Serve right away.

SAUCE PAIRINGS: *Traditionally, these gnocchi are paired with Tomato Sauce (page 175); Guanciale, Tomato, and Red Onion Sauce (page 176); Brown Butter with Sage (page 178); Fonduta (page 179); Gorgonzola Cream Sauce (page 180); Liver, Pancetta, and Porcini Ragù (page 181); Rabbit Ragù (page 182); Lamb Ragù (page 184); or Beef Ragù (page 186).*

BIETOLE (CHARD) GNOCCHI

SERVES 4

Bietole, or Swiss chard, is a common and favorite green throughout Italy. It is eaten as a contorni, *or vegetable side, as well as used in soups, dumplings, and tarts or pizza. Here,* bietole *adds a vegetal flavor to the potato dumpling, slightly lightening the texture.*

140 G/5 OZ SWISS CHARD, RIBS REMOVED
455 G/1 LB RUSSET OR YUKON GOLD POTATOES
1 EGG
1 TSP KOSHER SALT
FRESHLY GRATED NUTMEG
3 TBSP FINELY GRATED PARMIGIANO-REGGIANO CHEESE
150 G/1 CUP + 1 TBSP ALL-PURPOSE FLOUR, PLUS MORE AS NEEDED AND FOR DUSTING
SEMOLINA FLOUR FOR DUSTING
SAUCE OF YOUR CHOICE (SUGGESTIONS FOLLOW)

Prepare an ice bath by filling a large bowl with ice and cold water. Bring a large pot filled with generously salted water to a boil over medium-high heat. Add the chard and blanch until tender, about 2 minutes. Remove immediately from the pot with tongs and transfer to the ice bath. When cool, drain the chard in a colander. Place the chard in a kitchen towel and wring until mostly dry; a bit of residual moisture is fine. Finely chop and set aside.

In a medium pot, cover the potatoes with cold water. Bring to a simmer over medium-high heat and cook until the potatoes can be easily pierced with a skewer, 15 to 20 minutes. Drain the potatoes in a colander and set aside to cool.

When cool enough to handle, peel the potatoes and rice them into a large bowl. Add the chopped chard, egg, salt, a few swipes of nutmeg, the Parmigiano-Reggiano cheese,

and all-purpose flour and mix with your hands until the dough comes together. The dough should be soft but not sticky. Add more all-purpose flour, 1 Tbsp at a time, as needed to achieve this texture.

Sprinkle a small amount of all-purpose flour on a work surface, scrape all of the dough onto the surface, and top with another sprinkling of flour. This will help prevent the dough from being too sticky to roll.

Line a baking sheet with parchment paper and dust with semolina flour. Cut off a chunk of dough about the width of two fingers and cover the rest with plastic wrap. On a work surface lightly dusted with all-purpose flour, use your hands to roll the chunk into a log about ½ in (12 mm) in diameter. Do not incorporate too much more flour into the dough; add just enough so the dough does not stick to the surface. Cut the log into ½- to 1-in (12-mm to 2.5-cm) pieces. Put the gnocchi on the prepared baking sheet and shape the remaining dough. Make sure that the gnocchi don't touch or they will stick together.

(To store, refrigerate on the baking sheet, covered with plastic wrap, for up to 2 days, or freeze on the baking sheet and transfer to an airtight container. Use within 1 month. Do not thaw before cooking.)

Bring another large pot filled with generously salted water to a simmer over medium-high heat. Add the gnocchi and simmer until they float to the surface, 1 to 3 minutes. Remove immediately with a slotted spoon and finish with your choice of sauce. Serve right away.

SAUCE PAIRINGS: *These gnocchi are nicely complemented by Tomato Sauce (page 175); Guanciale, Tomato, and Red Onion Sauce (page 176); Brown Butter with Sage (page 178); Fonduta (page 179); Gorgonzola Cream Sauce (page 180); Liver, Pancetta, and Porcini Ragù (page 181); Rabbit Ragù (page 182); Lamb Ragù (page 184); and Beef Ragù (page 186).*

GNOCCHI OSSOLANI

SERVES 6

This delicious gnocchi dish from the Piedmont, specifically Val d'Ossola, is the pride of a mountain culture that's focused on artisanal butter and cheeses. These tender gnocchi always include squash, potato, and chestnut flour and are served with melted alpine pastured butter.

340 G/12 OZ RUSSET OR YUKON GOLD POTATOES
400 G/1⅔ CUPS SQUASH PURÉE (PAGE 191)
1 EGG YOLK
1 TBSP EXTRA-VIRGIN OLIVE OIL
1½ TSP KOSHER SALT
½ TSP FRESHLY GROUND BLACK PEPPER
½ SMALL NUTMEG, FRESHLY GRATED
100 G/¾ CUP ALL-PURPOSE FLOUR, PLUS MORE FOR DUSTING
100 G/1 CUP CHESTNUT FLOUR
SEMOLINA FLOUR FOR DUSTING
SAUCE OF YOUR CHOICE (SUGGESTIONS FOLLOW)

In a medium pot, cover the potatoes with cold water. Bring to a simmer over medium-high heat and cook until the potatoes can be easily pierced with a skewer, 15 to 20 minutes. Drain the potatoes in a colander and set aside to cool.

When cool enough to handle, peel the potatoes and rice them into a large bowl or the bowl of a stand mixer fitted with a paddle attachment. Add the squash purée, egg yolk, olive oil, salt, pepper, and nutmeg and mix with your hands or on medium speed until well blended, scraping down the sides of the bowl once or twice. Add the all-purpose flour and chestnut flour and mix with your

hands or on low speed just until combined. Do not overmix, as this will make the gnocchi tough. The dough should be soft and slightly sticky.

Dust 70 g/½ cup all-purpose flour on a work surface, then scrape the dough from the bowl directly on top of the flour. Sprinkle the top of the dough with an additional 70 g/½ cup flour. This will help prevent the dough from being too sticky to roll. Cover the dough with plastic wrap and let rest at room temperature for 10 minutes.

Line two baking sheets with parchment paper and dust with semolina flour. Cut off a chunk of dough about the width of two fingers and leave the rest covered with plastic wrap. On a work surface dusted with all-purpose flour, use your hands to roll the chunk into a log about ½ in (12 mm) in diameter. Cut the log into ¼-in (6-mm) pieces. Put the gnocchi on the prepared baking sheets and shape the remaining dough. Make sure that the gnocchi don't touch or they will stick together.

(To store, refrigerate on the baking sheets, covered with plastic wrap, for up to 2 days, or freeze on the baking sheets and transfer to an airtight container. Use within 1 month. Do not thaw before cooking.)

Bring a large pot filled with generously salted water to a simmer over medium-high heat. Add the gnocchi and simmer until they float to the surface, 1 to 3 minutes. Remove immediately with a slotted spoon and finish with your choice of sauce. Serve right away.

SAUCE PAIRINGS: *Traditionally, these gnocchi are paired with Brown Butter with Sage (page 178) or Fonduta (page 179).*

GNOCCHI ALLA BISMARK

SERVES 4

This simple gnocchi dish comes from the Piedmont and introduces prosciutto cotto (cured and cooked ham) into the dough, along with bread crumbs and flour. Similar to the style of canederli from farther north, these dumplings substitute fine dried bread crumbs for larger pieces and include a small amount of meat to add savor to the other inexpensive ingredients.

100 G/¾ CUP + 2 TBSP DRIED BREAD CRUMBS

200 G/1½ CUPS ALL-PURPOSE FLOUR, PLUS MORE FOR DUSTING

80 G/¾ CUP + 2 TBSP FINELY GRATED PARMIGIANO-REGGIANO CHEESE

1 EGG, PLUS 1 EGG YOLK

55 G/2 OZ PROSCIUTTO COTTO, FINELY CHOPPED

½ TSP GROUND CINNAMON

FRESHLY GRATED NUTMEG

1 TSP KOSHER SALT

100 G/¼ CUP + 3 TBSP WHOLE MILK, PLUS MORE AS NEEDED

SEMOLINA FLOUR FOR DUSTING

BROWN BUTTER WITH SAGE (PAGE 178)

In the bowl of a food processor, process the bread crumbs until finely ground.

In a medium bowl, combine the all-purpose flour, bread crumbs, and Parmigiano-Reggiano cheese. Add the egg, egg yolk, prosciutto cotto, cinnamon, a few swipes of nutmeg, and the salt and mix with your hands. Add the milk and stir with a wooden spoon to combine. Add more milk, 1 Tbsp at a time, until the dough comes together and is soft but not sticky. Transfer to a work surface and knead with your hands a few times, until the dough is cohesive. Cover the dough with plastic wrap and let rest at room temperature for 30 minutes.

Line a baking sheet with parchment paper and dust with semolina flour. Cut off a chunk of dough about the width of two fingers and cover the rest with plastic wrap. On a work surface lightly dusted with all-purpose flour, use your hands to roll the chunk into a log about ½ in (12 mm) in diameter. Cut the log into ½-in (12-mm) pieces. With the side of your thumb, gently push each piece against a gnocchi board or the back of the tines of a fork, rolling and flicking the dough to make a curled shape with an indentation on one side and a ridged surface on the other. Put the gnocchi on the prepared baking sheet and shape the remaining dough. Make sure that the gnocchi don't touch or they will stick together.

CONTINUED

(To store, refrigerate on the baking sheet, covered with plastic wrap, for up to 2 days, or freeze on the baking sheet and transfer to an airtight container. Use within 1 month. Do not thaw before cooking.)

Bring a large pot filled with generously salted water to a simmer over medium-high heat. Add the gnocchi and simmer until they float to the surface, 1 to 3 minutes. Remove immediately with a slotted spoon and finish with the brown butter. Serve right away.

BEET AND RICOTTA GNOCCHI

SERVES 6 TO 8

These beautiful gnocchi show off a rich red color. The flavor of the gnocchi is earthy but not intensely beet-y, and the texture is soft and delicate. This recipe is different from Beet and Potato Gnocchi (page 138), since it is enriched by the addition of ricotta cheese.

1.2 KG/2½ LB RED BEETS (WITHOUT GREENS), TRIMMED

KOSHER SALT AND FRESHLY GROUND BLACK PEPPER

2 TSP EXTRA-VIRGIN OLIVE OIL

¼ CUP (60 ML) WATER

1 EGG

240 G/1 CUP WHOLE-MILK RICOTTA CHEESE, HOMEMADE (SEE PAGE 190) OR STORE-BOUGHT

90 G/1 CUP FINELY GRATED PARMIGIANO-REGGIANO CHEESE

FRESHLY GRATED NUTMEG

420 G/3 CUPS ALL-PURPOSE FLOUR, PLUS MORE FOR DUSTING

SEMOLINA FLOUR FOR DUSTING

SAUCE OF YOUR CHOICE (SUGGESTIONS FOLLOW)

Preheat the oven to 350°F (180°C). Place the beets in a baking dish large enough to hold them in a single layer. Season lightly with salt and pepper, drizzle with the olive oil, and add the water. Cover the baking dish tightly with aluminum foil and roast until the beets can be easily pierced with a skewer, 40 to 60 minutes. Remove from the oven, uncover, and set aside to cool. When cool enough to handle, slip the skins off the beets with your fingers or a paring knife. Cut the beets into large chunks.

In a blender or the bowl of a food processor, combine the beets and egg and process until very smooth.

In a large bowl or the bowl of a stand mixer fitted with a paddle attachment, combine 340 g/1½ cups of the beet purée, the ricotta cheese, Parmigiano-Reggiano cheese, a few swipes of nutmeg, and 1 Tbsp salt. Mix with your hands or on medium speed until fully combined. Scrape down the sides of the bowl. Add the all-purpose flour and knead with your hands or on low speed just until combined. Do not overmix, as this will make the gnocchi tough. The dough should be soft and slightly sticky.

Dust 70 g/½ cup all-purpose flour on the work surface, then scrape the dough from the bowl directly on top of the flour. Lightly dust the top of the dough with more all-purpose flour. Cover the dough with plastic wrap and let rest at room temperature for 30 minutes.

CONTINUED

Line two baking sheets with parchment paper and dust with semolina flour. Cut off a chunk of dough about the width of two fingers and leave the rest covered with plastic wrap. On a work surface very lightly dusted with all-purpose flour, use your hands to roll the chunk into a log about ½ in (12 mm) in diameter. Cut the log into ¼-in (6-mm) pieces. Put the gnocchi on the prepared baking sheets and shape the remaining dough. Make sure that the gnocchi don't touch or they will stick together.

(To store, refrigerate on the baking sheets, covered with plastic wrap, for up to 2 days, or freeze on the baking sheets and transfer to an airtight container. Use within 1 month. Do not thaw before cooking.)

Bring a large pot filled with generously salted water to a simmer over medium-high heat. Add the gnocchi and simmer until they float to the surface, 1 to 3 minutes. Remove immediately with a slotted spoon and finish with your choice of sauce. Serve right away.

SAUCE PAIRINGS: *These pair well with Brown Butter with Sage (page 178), Fonduta (page 179), and Gorgonzola Cream Sauce (page 180).*

GNOCCHI WITH BEETS

When properly stored, beets keep beautifully through the winter, making them a handy ingredient when fresh produce is limited. Beet gnocchi can be made with or without potato. In addition to eggs and flour, potato or ricotta give tenderness to these sweet and earthy dumplings.

BEET AND POTATO GNOCCHI

SERVES 8

These gnocchi are from the Piedmont region in the north of Italy—an area known for its rich pastas (like pappardelle made with egg yolks instead of whole eggs), truffles, and hearty meat sauces. These beet gnocchi can be served with a rich sauce of Gorgonzola dolce and cream. I also like to serve them in a sage–brown butter sauce, along with some finely julienned beet greens that have been sautéed with olive oil and butter.

455 G/1 LB RED BEETS (WITHOUT GREENS), TRIMMED

KOSHER SALT AND FRESHLY GROUND BLACK PEPPER

2 TBSP EXTRA-VIRGIN OLIVE OIL

¼ CUP (60 ML) WATER

1 EGG, PLUS 1 EGG YOLK

240 G/8½ OZ RUSSET OR YUKON GOLD POTATOES

300 G/2 CUPS + 1 TBSP ALL-PURPOSE FLOUR, PLUS MORE AS NEEDED AND FOR DUSTING

½ SMALL NUTMEG, FRESHLY GRATED

SEMOLINA FLOUR FOR DUSTING

SAUCE OF YOUR CHOICE (SUGGESTIONS FOLLOW)

Preheat the oven to 350°F (180°C). Place the beets in a baking dish large enough to hold them in a single layer. Season lightly with salt and pepper, drizzle with the olive oil, and add the water. Cover the baking dish tightly with aluminum foil and roast until the beets can be easily pierced with a skewer, 40 to 60 minutes. Remove from the oven, uncover, and set aside to cool. When cool enough to handle, slip the skins off the beets with your fingers or a paring knife. Cut the beets into large chunks.

In a blender or the bowl of a food processor, combine the beets, egg, and egg yolk and process until very smooth.

In a medium pot, cover the potatoes with cold water. Bring to a simmer over medium-high heat and cook until the potatoes can be easily pierced with a skewer, 15 to 20 minutes. Drain the potatoes in a colander and set aside to cool.

When cool enough to handle, peel the potatoes and rice them into a large bowl. Add the beet purée, all-purpose flour, 1 tsp salt, and the nutmeg and mix with your hands until the dough comes together. The dough should be sticky and hold together in a ball. Add more flour, as needed, 1 Tbsp at a time, to achieve this texture.

Dust 70 g/½ cup all-purpose flour on the work surface, then scrape the dough from the bowl directly on top of the flour. Sprinkle the top of the dough with an additional 70 g/½ cup all-purpose flour. This will help prevent the dough from being too sticky to roll.

Line two baking sheets with parchment paper and dust with semolina flour. Cut off a chunk of dough about the width of two fingers and cover the rest with plastic wrap. On a work surface dusted with all-purpose flour, use your hands to roll the chunk into a log about ½ in (12 mm) in diameter. Do not incorporate too much more flour into the dough, adding just enough so the dough does not stick to the surface. Cut the log into ½- to 1-in (12-mm to 2.5-cm) pieces. Put the gnocchi on the prepared baking sheets and shape the remaining dough. Make sure that the gnocchi don't touch or they will stick together.

(To store, refrigerate on the baking sheets, covered with plastic wrap, for up to 2 days, or freeze on the baking sheets and transfer to an airtight container. Use within 1 month. Do not thaw before cooking.)

Bring a large pot filled with generously salted water to a simmer over medium-high heat. Add the gnocchi and simmer until they float to the surface, 1 to 3 minutes. Remove immediately with a slotted spoon and finish with your choice of sauce. Serve right away.

SAUCE PAIRINGS: *These pair well with Brown Butter with Sage (page 178), Fonduta (page 179), and Gorgonzola Cream Sauce (page 180).*

POTATO AND SCULPIT GNOCCHI

SERVES 8

Sculpit, also known as stridolo, *is an herb most commonly used in northern Italy's pasta and risotto dishes. It grows in gardens, fields, forests, and mountains and tastes grassy and similar to chicories, or bitter greens. Sculpit is harvested as a leaf, before the first blooms appear. This unique recipe includes a purée of onion and sculpit that's folded into the potato base, yielding a tender and very flavorful gnocchi.*

1.4 KG/3 LB RUSSET OR YUKON GOLD POTATOES

KOSHER SALT

¼ CUP (60 ML) EXTRA-VIRGIN OLIVE OIL

1 LARGE YELLOW ONION, THINLY SLICED

60 G/2 CUPS LOOSELY PACKED SCULPIT LEAVES

3 EGGS

85 G/½ CUP + 2 TBSP ALL-PURPOSE FLOUR, PLUS MORE FOR DUSTING

SAUCE OF YOUR CHOICE (SUGGESTIONS FOLLOW)

Peel the potatoes and cut them into 1-in (2.5-cm) cubes. Place the potatoes in a medium pot, cover with cold water, and season with salt. Bring to a simmer over medium-high heat and cook until the potatoes are tender but not falling apart, about 10 minutes. Drain the potatoes in a colander and let sit in the colander for a few minutes to expel any additional moisture. In a medium bowl, mash the potatoes coarsely with a whisk and then allow to cool just long enough so that they can be handled. There should not be any potato pieces larger than a pea.

In a medium sauté pan, warm the olive oil over medium heat. Add the onion and sculpit and sauté until the onion is translucent but not browned, 6 to 8 minutes. Season with salt.

Transfer the onion mixture to the bowl of a food processor and process until finely blended. Add the onion mixture, eggs, 1 Tbsp salt, and flour to the potatoes and mix gently with your hands just until the dough comes together. The dough should be soft, sticky, and very wet. Do not overmix, as this will make the gnocchi tough.

Dust 30 g/¼ cup flour on the work surface, then scrape the dough from the bowl directly on top of the flour. Sprinkle the top of the dough with an additional 30 g/¼ cup flour. This will help prevent the dough from being too sticky to roll.

Line two baking sheets with parchment paper and dust with flour. Cut off a chunk of dough about the width of two fingers and cover the rest with plastic wrap.

On a work surface generously dusted with flour, use your hands to roll the chunk into a log about ½ in (12 mm) in diameter. Do not incorporate too much more flour into the dough, adding just enough so that the dough does not stick to the surface. Cut the log into ½- to 1-in (12-mm to 2.5-cm) pieces. If any pieces of potato larger than a pea remain, remove and discard them. Put the gnocchi on the prepared baking sheets and shape the remaining dough. Make sure that the gnocchi don't touch or they will stick together.

Refrigerate on the baking sheets, covered with plastic wrap, for at least 8 hours, or up to overnight; after about 4 hours, use a bench scraper to gently flip the gnocchi to coat the second sides with flour and make sure that the gnocchi do not stick to the parchment paper. This delicate-textured gnocchi is best if refrigerated overnight; this gives the dumplings time to dry and set up nicely.

(For longer storage, refrigerate on the baking sheets, covered with plastic wrap, for up to 2 days, or freeze on the baking sheets and transfer to an airtight container. Use within 1 month. Do not thaw before cooking.)

Bring a large pot filled with generously salted water to a simmer over medium-high heat. Using a pastry brush, dust excess flour from the gnocchi and add them to the water. Simmer until they float to the surface, 1 to 3 minutes. Remove immediately with a slotted spoon and finish with your choice of sauce. Serve right away.

SAUCE PAIRINGS: *Traditionally, these gnocchi are paired with Brown Butter with Sage (page 178); Liver, Pancetta, and Porcini Ragù (page 181); Rabbit Ragù (page 182); Lamb Ragù (page 184); or Beef Ragù (page 186).*

CHESTNUT GNOCCHI

SERVES 6

Castagna *is the Italian word for "chestnut," and the dense texture and sweet flavor of chestnut flour set castagna gnocchi apart from other dumplings. The dough can be made with a combination of wheat flour and chestnut flour, or with the addition of potatoes. The dough should be very soft but not sticky. Castagna gnocchi have a rich and nutty aroma when cooked.*

455 G/1 LB RUSSET OR YUKON GOLD POTATOES
310 G/3 CUPS + 2 TBSP CHESTNUT FLOUR
140 G/1 CUP ALL-PURPOSE FLOUR, PLUS MORE FOR DUSTING
1½ TSP KOSHER SALT
1 EGG
150 G/⅔ CUP WARM WATER
SEMOLINA FLOUR FOR DUSTING
SAUCE OF YOUR CHOICE (SUGGESTIONS FOLLOW)

In a medium pot, cover the potatoes with cold water. Bring the water to a simmer over medium-high heat and cook until the potatoes can be easily pierced with a skewer, 15 to 20 minutes. Drain the potatoes in a colander and set aside to cool.

Sift together the chestnut flour and all-purpose flour into a large bowl. Stir in the salt.

When the potatoes are cool enough to handle, peel and rice them into the bowl with the flours. Add the egg and mix by hand until fully combined. Stir in the warm water, 2 to 3 Tbsp at a time, until the dough is cohesive. Transfer to a work surface dusted with all-purpose flour and knead a few times until the dough is cohesive and soft without being sticky.

Line two baking sheets with parchment paper and dust with semolina flour. Cut off a chunk of dough about the width of two fingers and cover the rest with plastic wrap. On a work surface lightly dusted with all-purpose flour, use your hands to roll the chunk into a log about ½ in (12 mm) in diameter. Do not incorporate too much more flour into the dough, adding just enough so that the dough does not stick to the surface. Cut the log into ½- to 1-in (12-mm to 2.5-cm) pieces. Put the gnocchi on the prepared baking sheets and shape the remaining dough. Make sure that the gnocchi don't touch or they will stick together.

(To store, refrigerate on the baking sheets, covered with plastic wrap, for up to 2 days, or freeze on the baking sheets and transfer to an airtight container. Use within 1 month. Do not thaw before cooking.)

Bring a large pot filled with generously salted water to a simmer over medium-high heat. Add the gnocchi and simmer until they float to the surface, about 1 to 3 minutes.

Continue to simmer until tender, about 3 minutes more. Chestnut flour is very dense, so these dumplings require extra cooking time. Remove immediately with a slotted spoon and finish with your choice of sauce. Serve right away.

SAUCE PAIRINGS: *Traditionally, these gnocchi are paired with Guanciale, Tomato, and Red Onion Sauce (page 176); Brown Butter with Sage (page 178); Fonduta (page 179); or Gorgonzola Cream Sauce (page 180).*

GNOCCHI VICENZA

SERVES 4

Whenever I visit Venice, I quickly notice a connection between Venetians and the consumption of the Italian eau-de-vie known as grappa. Nonnas drink grappa on their way to the market in the morning and everyone—myself included—drinks it after a meal. Venetians are proud of their tradition of grappa distillation, and they embrace the influence of other cultures brought in from their seaports. This dish is deeply inflected by ingredients from other shores.

Be sure to gently warm this sauce. Simmering or boiling will cause it to caramelize and break apart.

1 CUP (120 G) GOLDEN RAISINS

¾ CUP (170 G) UNSALTED BUTTER

¼ CUP (50 G) SUGAR

2½ TBSP GROUND CINNAMON

3 TBSP GRAPPA

KOSHER SALT

1 RECIPE GNOCCHI WITH EGG AND RICOTTA (PAGE 96), UNCOOKED

In a small bowl, plump the raisins in boiling water to cover. Allow to sit for 5 minutes, then drain.

In a large sauté pan, melt the butter over low heat. Add the sugar and cinnamon, stir to combine, and cook for 2 to 3 minutes, until the mixture resembles soft caramel. Add the raisins and grappa and lightly season with salt. Gently warm the sauce for 30 seconds (do not let it simmer or boil, as it will become gluey and break apart), then remove from the heat.

Bring a large pot filled with generously salted water to a simmer over medium-high heat. Add the gnocchi and simmer until they float to the surface, 1 to 3 minutes. Remove immediately with a slotted spoon and add to the sauce. Stir gently to coat the gnocchi with the sauce. Serve right away.

GNOCCHI ALLA VALDOSTANA

SERVES 4

Fontina Val d'Aosta is a rich and earthy semifirm cheese from the Aosta Valley in Italy. It is a celebrated ingredient in the region's cuisine and adds a delicious flavor, texture, and general savory quality to this special dumpling.

430 G/15 OZ RUSSET OR YUKON GOLD POTATOES

75 G/½ CUP + 1 TBSP ALL-PURPOSE FLOUR, PLUS MORE AS NEEDED AND FOR DUSTING

45 G/½ CUP FINELY GRATED PARMIGIANO-REGGIANO CHEESE

55 G/2 OZ FONTINA VAL D'AOSTA CHEESE, CUT INTO VERY TINY CUBES

1 EGG YOLK

1 TSP KOSHER SALT

SEMOLINA FLOUR FOR DUSTING

SAUCE OF YOUR CHOICE (SUGGESTIONS FOLLOW)

In a medium pot, cover the potatoes with cold water. Bring to a simmer over medium-high heat and cook the potatoes until they can be easily pierced with a skewer, 15 to 20 minutes. Drain the potatoes in a colander and set aside to cool.

When cool enough to handle, peel the potatoes and rice them into a large bowl. Add the all-purpose flour, Parmigiano-Reggiano cheese, Fontina cheese, egg yolk, and salt and mix with your hands until the dough comes together. The dough should be soft but not sticky. Add more all-purpose flour as needed, 1 Tbsp at a time, to achieve this texture.

Dust a work surface with a small amount of all-purpose flour, scrape the dough onto the surface, and top with another sprinkling of all-purpose flour. This will help prevent the dough from being too sticky to roll.

Line a baking sheet with parchment paper and dust with semolina flour. Cut off a chunk of dough about the width of two fingers and cover the rest with plastic wrap. On a work surface very lightly dusted with all-purpose flour, use your hands to roll the chunk into a log about ½ in (12 mm) in diameter. Do not incorporate too much more flour into the dough, adding just enough so the dough does not stick to the surface. Cut the log into ½- to 1-in (12-mm to 2.5-cm) pieces. Put the gnocchi on the prepared baking sheet and shape the remaining dough. Make sure that the gnocchi don't touch or they will stick together.

(To store, refrigerate on the baking sheet, covered with plastic wrap, for up to 2 days, or freeze on the baking sheet and transfer to an airtight container. Use within 1 month. Do not thaw before cooking.)

Bring a large pot filled with generously salted water to a simmer over medium-high heat. Add the gnocchi and simmer until they float to the surface, 1 to 3 minutes. Remove immediately with a slotted spoon and finish with your choice of sauce. Serve right away.

SAUCE PAIRINGS: *Traditionally, these gnocchi are paired with Pesto (page 172); Tomato Sauce (page 175); Guanciale, Tomato, and Red Onion Sauce (page 176); Brown Butter with Sage (page 178); Fonduta (page 179); Gorgonzola Cream Sauce (page 180); Liver, Pancetta, and Porcini Ragù (page 181); Rabbit Ragù (page 182); Lamb Ragù (page 184); or Beef Ragù (page 186).*

GNOCCHI ALLA BAVA

SERVES 4

Traditional to Val d'Aosta, gnocchi alla bava *is the name of the prepared dish, not the specific gnocchi.* Bava, *meaning "drool," refers to the stringy strands of cheese that are melted but not smooth. The gnocchi can be made of potato or buckwheat flour, but the sauce always features Fontina Val d'Aosta, the local alpine cheese. The texture of this gnocchi is denser than potato gnocchi, but it should not be tough.*

200 G/1½ CUPS ALL-PURPOSE FLOUR, PLUS MORE FOR DUSTING
200 G/1½ CUPS BUCKWHEAT FLOUR
1¾ TSP KOSHER SALT
230 G/1 CUP WATER
SEMOLINA FLOUR FOR DUSTING
FONDUTA (PAGE 179)

In a medium bowl, combine the all-purpose flour, buckwheat flour, and salt. Slowly stir in the water. Knead with your hands until the dough is soft but not too sticky, about 5 minutes. Transfer to a work surface dusted with all-purpose flour and knead a few times to create a cohesive mass. Cover the dough with plastic wrap and let rest at room temperature for 30 minutes.

Line a baking sheet with parchment paper and dust with semolina flour. Cut off a chunk of dough about the width of two fingers and cover the rest with plastic wrap. On a work surface lightly dusted with all-purpose flour, use your hands to roll the chunk into a log about ½ in (12-mm) in diameter. Do not incorporate too much more flour into the dough, adding just enough so that the dough does not stick to the surface.

Cut the log into ½- to 1-in (12-mm to 2.5-cm) pieces. Put the gnocchi on the prepared baking sheet and shape the remaining dough. Make sure that the gnocchi don't touch or they will stick together.

(To store, refrigerate on the baking sheet, covered with plastic wrap, for up to 2 days, or freeze on the baking sheet and transfer to an airtight container. Use within 1 month. Do not thaw before cooking.)

Bring a large pot filled with generously salted water to a simmer over medium-high heat. Add the gnocchi and simmer until they float to the surface, 1 to 3 minutes. Continue to simmer until tender, 3 to 4 minutes more. These dumplings are denser than most gnocchi, so they require extra cooking time. Remove immediately with a slotted spoon and finish with the fonduta. Serve right away.

TRADITIONAL SPÄTZLI
SERVES 6

This traditional recipe for a basic spätzli can be altered in various ways to change the flavor and texture. Replace half of the all-purpose flour with whole-wheat flour for what the Italians call integrale. Or add chopped thyme, parsley, or oregano for an herbed spätzli.

350 G/2½ CUPS ALL-PURPOSE FLOUR
2 TSP KOSHER SALT
2 EGGS
300 G/1¼ CUPS WHOLE MILK, PLUS MORE AS NEEDED
EXTRA-VIRGIN OLIVE OIL FOR TOSSING
SAUCE OF YOUR CHOICE (SUGGESTIONS FOLLOW)

In a large bowl or the bowl of a stand mixer fitted with a paddle attachment, combine the flour, salt, eggs, and milk. Mix with a wooden spoon or on medium speed until just combined, 3 to 4 minutes. Stir more vigorously or raise the speed up a notch or two and beat until the batter becomes slightly shiny and elastic, 3 to 5 minutes. Cover the bowl with plastic wrap and let rest at room temperature for 30 minutes.

After 30 minutes, check the texture of the batter—it should be thin and elastic, with more stretch than a typical batter. If it is too thick, add more milk, 1 Tbsp at a time, to achieve this texture.

Line a baking sheet with parchment paper. Bring a large pot filled with generously salted water to a simmer over medium-high heat. Working in batches, press the dough through a spätzli maker or colander into the simmering water. Simmer the spätzli until they float to the surface, about 1 minute. Stir to release any spätzli that have settled on the bottom of the pot. Simmer for 1 minute more, until tender. Remove immediately with a fine-mesh strainer and transfer to the prepared baking sheet. Toss the cooked spätzli with a little olive oil, so they don't stick together. Allow to cool to room temperature. Finish with your choice of sauce. Serve right away.

SAUCE PAIRINGS: *Use these spätzli in Spätzli with Sage and Speck (page 154) or serve with Brown Butter with Sage (page 178).*

SPINACH SPÄTZLI

SERVES 4

The Germanic and Austrian influences in northern Italy are evident in its cuisine. Dishes like stru-del and spätzli have become typical fare for the regions of Trentino-Alto Adige and Südtirol. This spinach spätzli is soft, tender, and simple to make. I learned this recipe from Gianna, a wonderful home cook from outside of Trento. She explained that she uses frozen spinach since very little grows year-round in her area. The intense winters make for a simple cuisine using the best of whatever foods are available. Traditionally, these spätzli are used in Spätzli with Sage and Speck.

910 G/2 LB FRESH SPINACH, STEMMED

4 EGGS

¼ NUTMEG, FRESHLY GRATED

1 TSP KOSHER SALT

280 G/2 CUPS ALL-PURPOSE FLOUR

Prepare an ice bath by filling a large bowl with ice and cold water. Bring a large pot filled with generously salted water to a boil over medium-high heat. Add the spinach and blanch until wilted, about 2 minutes. Remove immediately from the pot with tongs and transfer to the ice bath. When cool, drain the spinach in a colander. Place the spinach in a kitchen towel and wring until mostly dry; a bit of residual moisture is fine.

In the bowl of a food processor, com-bine the spinach, eggs, nutmeg, and salt and process for about 2 minutes, until the spinach is broken up and mostly chopped. Add the flour and process for about 4 minutes, scrap-ing down the sides of the bowl as needed. The batter should be thick and smooth. (If it

is too thick, add water, 1 tsp at a time.) Lightly oil a medium bowl and transfer the batter to the bowl. Cover with plastic wrap and let rest at room temperature for 30 minutes.

Line a baking sheet with parchment paper. Bring another large pot filled with generously salted water to a simmer over medium-high heat. Working in batches, press the dough through a spätzli maker or colander into the simmering water. Simmer the spätzli until they float to the surface, about 1 minute. Stir to release any spätzli that have settled on the bottom of the pot. Simmer for 1 minute more, until tender. Remove immediately with a fine-mesh strainer and transfer to the prepared baking sheet. Let cool to room temperature. Serve right away.

BEET SPÄTZLI

SERVES 6

This tender dumpling is traditionally found throughout many northern Italian mountainous regions. It is a simple dough featuring a small amount of fresh beets, which can be stored throughout the long winter season. Since the growing season is so short and the winters are so intense, mountain cultures rely on starch, dairy (protein-rich cheeses), and limited meat for the foundation of their diet. Dried mushrooms and root vegetables like beets that can be cellared often garnish dishes.

455 G/1 LB RED BEETS (WITHOUT GREENS), TRIMMED

KOSHER SALT AND FRESHLY GROUND BLACK PEPPER

2 TBSP EXTRA-VIRGIN OLIVE OIL

¼ CUP (60 ML) WATER

2 EGGS

320 G/2¼ CUPS ALL-PURPOSE FLOUR

BROWN BUTTER WITH SAGE (PAGE 178)

Preheat the oven to 350°F (180°C). Place the beets in a baking dish large enough to hold them in a single layer. Season lightly with salt and pepper, drizzle with the olive oil, and add the water. Cover the baking dish tightly with aluminum foil and roast until the beets can be easily pierced with a skewer, 40 to 60 minutes. Remove from the oven, uncover, and set aside to cool. When cool enough to handle, slip the skins off the beets with your fingers or a paring knife. Cut the beets into large chunks.

In a blender or the bowl of a food processor, combine the beets and eggs and process until smooth, scraping down the sides of the bowl as needed. Add the flour and 1 Tbsp salt and process until a thick batter forms.

Line a baking sheet with parchment paper. Bring a large pot filled with generously salted water to a simmer over medium-high heat. Working in batches, press the batter through a spätzli maker or colander into the simmering water. Simmer the spätzli until they float to the surface, about 1 minute. Stir to release any spätzli that have settled on the bottom of the pot. Simmer for 1 minute more, until tender. Remove immediately with a fine-mesh strainer and transfer to the prepared baking sheet. Let cool to room temperature. Finish with the brown butter. Serve right away.

SPÄTZLI WITH SAGE AND SPECK

SERVES 4 TO 6

This simple preparation is a staple in the alpine region of Italy. The few basics of butter, Parmigiano-Reggiano, and speck (a smoked and cured ham) are widely available, even during the winter months when fresh produce is sparse.

115 G/8 TBSP UNSALTED BUTTER

6 FRESH SAGE LEAVES

8 THIN SLICES SPECK, CUT INTO NARROW RIBBONS

1 RECIPE TRADITIONAL SPÄTZLI (PAGE 151), SPINACH SPÄTZLI (PAGE 152), OR BEET SPÄTZLI (PAGE 153)

KOSHER SALT AND FRESHLY GROUND BLACK PEPPER

GRATED PARMIGIANO-REGGIANO CHEESE FOR SERVING

In a large sauté pan, heat the butter and sage until the butter melts. Add the speck and toss to coat with the butter. Remove the pan from the heat, add the spätzli, and toss to combine. Season with salt and pepper. Spoon into serving bowls and top with grated Parmigiano-Reggiano cheese. Serve right away.

GNOCCHI DI CIADIN

SERVES 6

The name gnocchi di ciadin *refers to the bowl—called a* ciadin—*that the dough is traditionally mixed in. A long wooden spoon—known as a* mistolo—*with a wide, flat beating end, is used to mix the dough. Similar to spätzli, gnocchi di ciadin is made with a wet and elastic dough that yields tender dumplings. Traditionally, a portion of the dough is placed onto a rectangular wooden board and small dollops of dough are scraped into simmering water. Modern-day cooks use a spätzli maker (see page 21) for more efficient production. Some chefs and home cooks replace the traditional smoked ricotta with grana or Parmigiano-Reggiano cheese. The dough oxidizes quickly, turning a grayish color, so cooking the batter within six hours of making it is recommended.*

1½ LB (650 G) RED POTATOES

⅓ CUP + 2 TBSP (55 G) DRIED BREAD CRUMBS

4 EGGS

300 G/1¼ CUPS WHOLE MILK, PLUS MORE AS NEEDED

4 TSP KOSHER SALT

600 G/4¼ CUPS ALL-PURPOSE FLOUR

¼ CUP (25 G) FINELY GRATED SMOKED RICOTTA SALATA CHEESE OR PARMIGIANO-REGGIANO CHEESE

1 CUP (240 ML) BROWN BUTTER WITH SAGE (PAGE 178), WARM

In a medium pot, cover the potatoes with cold water. Bring to a simmer over medium-high heat and cook until the potatoes can be easily pierced with a skewer, 15 to 20 minutes. Drain the potatoes in a colander and set aside to cool. When cool enough to handle, peel the potatoes, cut them into ¼-in (6-mm) slices, and set aside.

In the bowl of a food processor, process the bread crumbs until finely ground. Transfer to a small bowl and set aside until ready to serve.

In a large bowl, break up the eggs with a whisk. Add the milk and salt and whisk to combine. Add the flour and stir vigorously with a wooden spoon until the dough has the consistency of a thick, elastic pancake batter. If it is too thick, add more milk, 1 Tbsp at a time. Vigorous stirring will build gluten, giving the gnocchi texture. This dough doesn't need to rest.

Bring a large pot filled with generously salted water to a gentle simmer over medium-high heat. Drop the batter, 1 Tbsp at a time, into the simmering water, then add the potato slices. After the gnocchi float to the surface, cook for 1 minute more, gently stirring to keep the gnocchi from sticking together.

Remove the gnocchi and potatoes immediately with a slotted spoon and divide among six bowls. Top with the smoked ricotta salata and bread crumbs and drizzle with the Brown Butter with Sage to serve.

BUCKWHEAT AND RICOTTA GNOCCHI

SERVES 8

Buckwheat is prevalent in alpine cuisine. The grain is able to flourish in rugged terrain, making it a great crop for the short growing season. The earthy flavor of buckwheat pairs well with the region's smoked cheeses and meats, which are typically all that is available during the winter months.

455 G/1¾ CUPS + 2 TBSP WHOLE-MILK RICOTTA CHEESE, HOMEMADE (SEE PAGE 190) OR STORE-BOUGHT

4 EGG YOLKS

FRESHLY GRATED NUTMEG

2 TSP KOSHER SALT

¼ TSP FRESHLY GROUND BLACK PEPPER

30 G/⅓ CUP GRATED AGED PECORINO CHEESE

170 G/1 CUP + 3 TBSP ALL-PURPOSE FLOUR, PLUS MORE FOR DUSTING

120 G/¾ CUP + 2 TBSP BUCKWHEAT FLOUR

SEMOLINA FLOUR FOR DUSTING

SAUCE OF YOUR CHOICE (SUGGESTIONS FOLLOW)

In a large bowl or the bowl of a stand mixer fitted with a paddle attachment, mix together the ricotta cheese, egg yolks, a few swipes of nutmeg, salt, pepper, and pecorino cheese. Scrape down the sides of the bowl. Add the all-purpose flour and buckwheat flour and knead with your hands or on low speed just until combined. Do not overmix, as this will make the gnocchi tough.

Line two baking sheets with parchment paper and dust with semolina flour. Cut off a chunk of dough about the width of two fingers and cover the rest with plastic wrap.

On a work surface dusted with all-purpose flour, use your hands to roll the chunk into a log that is ½ in (12 mm) in diameter. Cut the log into ¼-in (6-mm) pieces. Put the gnocchi on the prepared baking sheets and shape the remaining dough. Make sure that the gnocchi don't touch or they will stick together.

Bring a large pot filled with generously salted water to a simmer over medium-high heat. Add the gnocchi and simmer until they float to the surface, 1 to 3 minutes. Remove immediately with a slotted spoon and finish with your choice of sauce. Serve right away.

SAUCE PAIRINGS: *These gnocchi are traditionally served with Guanciale, Tomato, and Red Onion Sauce (page 176); Brown Butter with Sage (page 178); Fonduta (page 179); Gorgonzola Cream Sauce (page 180); Liver, Pancetta, and Porcini Ragù (page 181); Rabbit Ragù (page 182); Lamb Ragù (page 184); or Beef Ragù (page 186).*

GNOCCHI WITH DRIED NETTLES

SERVES 4

Ortica is the Italian word for "nettle," and the vegetable is used throughout many regions of Italy, most often in its fresh form in the spring months. These dumplings feature dried nettles, which are used during the long winter months when little fresh produce is available, and stale bread, the backbone of cucina povera, *or the "cuisine of the poor." Dried nettles are difficult to find in the United States, so the next time you're in Italy, bring some home with you—they're easy to stash in a suitcase.*

230 G/1 CUP WATER

300 G/10½ OZ STALE BREAD, CUT INTO SMALL CUBES

2 TBSP DRIED NETTLES

1 EGG

50 G/½ CUP + 1 TBSP FINELY GRATED PARMIGIANO-REGGIANO CHEESE, PLUS MORE FOR SERVING

KOSHER SALT AND FRESHLY GROUND BLACK PEPPER

3 TBSP + 1 TSP ALL-PURPOSE FLOUR, PLUS MORE FOR ROLLING

4 TBSP (55 G) UNSALTED BUTTER, MELTED

Bring the water to a boil over high heat. In a medium bowl, combine the bread with the boiling water, using just enough to soften the bread; there should be no pooling in the bottom of the bowl. Gently mix the bread and water with a wooden spoon. Add the nettles, egg, and Parmigiano-Reggiano cheese and mix well. The bread cubes should soften and break apart. Season lightly with salt and pepper. Add the flour and gently knead in the bowl with your hands or transfer to a lightly floured work surface and knead until the dough is smooth and soft. Cover with plastic wrap and refrigerate for 30 minutes.

Line a baking sheet with parchment paper. Put 140 g/1 cup flour in a shallow bowl. With your hands or a small ice-cream scoop, scoop 3 to 4 Tbsp of dough and gently form into a ball. Roll the ball in the flour to lightly coat and place on the prepared baking sheet. Repeat with the remaining dough. Make sure that the gnocchi don't touch or they will stick together.

Bring a large pot filled with generously salted water to a simmer over medium-high heat. Add the gnocchi and simmer for 3 to 4 minutes, then remove one with a slotted spoon and taste for tenderness. If the gnocco is still firm in the center, simmer for 1 to 2 minutes more, until tender throughout. Remove immediately with a slotted spoon to four bowls and finish with the melted butter and a grating of Parmigiano-Reggiano cheese. Serve right away.

STRANGOLAPRETI

SERVES 6

In the north of Italy, this dumpling goes by the name strangolapreti, *and in the south, it is known as* strozzapreti. *Traditionally, strangolapreti from Trento is made with grana Trentino, a hard cow's milk cheese from the region. The Messina family, who taught me to make this dumpling, prefers the taste of Parmigiano-Reggiano cheese and substitute it in this recipe. In tougher times, poorer families would omit the ricotta cheese, which is a more costly ingredient. Strangolapreti are typically served in broth, or can be served with melted butter.*

500 G/18 OZ FRESH SPINACH, STEMMED

85 G/3 OZ STALE BREAD, CUT INTO ¼-IN (6-MM) CUBES

155 G/½ CUP + 2 TBSP WHOLE MILK, PLUS MORE AS NEEDED

2 EGGS

2 TBSP WHOLE-MILK RICOTTA CHEESE, HOMEMADE (SEE PAGE 190) OR STORE-BOUGHT

45 G/½ CUP FINELY GRATED PARMIGIANO-REGGIANO CHEESE, PLUS MORE FOR SERVING

1 TSP KOSHER SALT

FRESHLY GRATED NUTMEG

75 G/½ CUP + 1 TBSP ALL-PURPOSE FLOUR, PLUS MORE AS NEEDED AND FOR DUSTING

6 TBSP (85 G) UNSALTED BUTTER, MELTED

Prepare an ice bath by filling a large bowl with ice and cold water. Bring a large pot filled with generously salted water to a boil over medium-high heat. Add the spinach and blanch until wilted, about 2 minutes. Remove immediately from the pot with tongs and transfer to the ice bath. When cool, drain the spinach in a colander. Place the spinach in a kitchen towel and wring until mostly dry; a bit of residual moisture is fine. Finely chop and set aside.

In a large bowl, moisten the bread with the milk and let stand for a few minutes to allow the bread to soften and absorb the milk; the bread should be fully saturated but there should be no pooling in the bottom of the bowl. If needed, add more milk, 1 Tbsp at a time. Let rest at room temperature for 30 minutes.

Using your hands, thoroughly break apart the moistened bread until no big pieces remain. Add the spinach, eggs, ricotta cheese, and Parmigiano-Reggiano cheese and mix well. Stir in the salt and a few swipes of nutmeg. Add the flour and stir just until combined.

Bring another large pot filled with generously salted water to a simmer over medium-high heat. Drop 1 Tbsp of the dough into the simmering water and cook for 2 to 4 minutes. If the dough does not hold its shape, add a bit more flour, as needed, 1 Tbsp at a time, to the dough and test again. This is a delicate dumpling; the goal is to add only as much flour as needed to the dough to get the dumplings to maintain their shape.

Dust two baking sheets with flour.

Put 140 g/1 cup flour in a shallow bowl. With your fingers, pull off walnut-size pieces of dough. Working with one piece at a time, gently roll in the flour to lightly coat. Put the strangolapreti on the prepared baking sheets. Make sure that the strangolapreti don't touch or they will stick together.

(To store, refrigerate on the baking sheets, covered with plastic wrap, for up to 2 days, or freeze on the baking sheets and transfer to an airtight container. Use within 1 month. Do not thaw before cooking.)

Working in three batches, add the strangolapreti to the simmering water and cook until they float to the surface, 1 to 3 minutes. Remove immediately with a slotted spoon to individual bowls and finish with the melted butter and a grating of Parmigiano-Reggiano cheese. Serve right away.

STRANGOLAPRETI WITH BREAD CRUMBS

SERVES 4

These dumplings are dense and hearty, and so good. They are unique in that they are made with finely ground bread crumbs instead of stale bread cubes. The high ratio of greens to bread suggests a dumpling made in summer, when produce is more readily available. Ladle hot chicken stock (see page 189) over the dumplings to serve as a soup.

60 G/½ CUP DRIED BREAD CRUMBS

280 G/10 OZ FRESH SPINACH, STEMMED

1 EGG

¼ TSP KOSHER SALT

¼ TSP FRESHLY GROUND BLACK PEPPER

FRESHLY GRATED NUTMEG

30 G/⅓ CUP FINELY GRATED AGED PECORINO CHEESE

45 G/⅓ CUP ALL-PURPOSE FLOUR, PLUS MORE FOR DUSTING AND ROLLING

4 TBSP (55 G) UNSALTED BUTTER, MELTED

FINELY GRATED PARMIGIANO-REGGIANO CHEESE FOR SERVING

In the bowl of a food processor, process the bread crumbs until finely ground and set aside.

Prepare an ice bath by filling a large bowl with ice and cold water. Bring a large pot filled with generously salted water to a boil over medium-high heat. Add the spinach and blanch until wilted, about 2 minutes. Remove immediately from the pot with tongs and transfer to the ice bath. When cool, drain the spinach in a colander. Place the spinach in a kitchen towel and wring until mostly dry; a bit of residual moisture is fine.

Finely chop the spinach and place in a medium bowl. Add the egg, salt, pepper, a few swipes of nutmeg, the pecorino cheese,

and bread crumbs and mix with your hands just until combined. Add the flour and gently knead until thoroughly combined.

Line a baking sheet with parchment paper and lightly dust with flour. Put 70 g/ ½ cup flour in a shallow bowl. Using two tablespoons, scoop up enough dough to make a dumpling just a little smaller than a golf ball. With your hands, gently roll the dough into a compact ball, then gently roll in the flour to lightly coat. Put the strangolapreti on the prepared baking sheet and shape the remaining dough, rolling each ball in flour. Make sure that the strangolapreti don't touch or they will stick together.

When all the strangolapreti have been formed, gently shake the baking sheet and roll the pasta around in the flour until all sides are coated with flour. Refrigerate, uncovered, for at least 1 hour.

(To store, refrigerate on the baking sheet, covered with plastic wrap, for up to 2 days, or freeze on the baking sheet and transfer to an airtight container. Use within 1 month. Do not thaw before cooking.)

Bring another large pot filled with generously salted water to a simmer over medium-high heat. Add the strangolapreti and simmer until tender, 1 to 3 minutes; they will not float to the surface like gnocchi. Remove immediately with a slotted spoon to four individual bowls and finish with the melted butter and a grating of Parmigiano-Reggiano cheese. Serve right away.

CANEDERLI

SERVES 6

These traditional canederli are typical in Trento. The garnishes of sausage and speck feature left-overs that a family might have readily available in their refrigerator. Grana Trentino is the cheese traditionally used in this area, but the Messina family, who taught me to make these dumplings, prefer Parmigiano-Reggiano to the local cheese. Lucanica is the local pork sausage that is gently flavored with garlic.

115 G/4 OZ STALE BREAD, CUT INTO ¼-IN (6-MM) CUBES

170 G/½ CUP + 3 TBSP WHOLE MILK, WARM, PLUS MORE AS NEEDED

2 TBSP EXTRA-VIRGIN OLIVE OIL

½ YELLOW ONION, CUT INTO SMALL DICE

1 GARLIC CLOVE, MINCED

1 TBSP CHOPPED FRESH ITALIAN PARSLEY

55 G/2 OZ SPECK, CUT INTO SMALL DICE

100 G/3½ OZ LUCANICA OR OTHER MILD PORK SAUSAGE, CASING REMOVED

1 EGG

100 G/¾ CUP ALL-PURPOSE FLOUR, PLUS MORE FOR ROLLING

KOSHER SALT

8 CUPS (2 L) CHICKEN STOCK (PAGE 189)

PARMIGIANO-REGGIANO CHEESE FOR GRATING

In a large bowl, moisten the bread with the milk and let stand for a few minutes to allow the bread to soften and absorb the milk; the bread should be fully saturated but there should be no pooling in the bottom of the bowl. If needed, add more milk, 1 Tbsp at a time.

In a medium sauté pan, warm the olive oil over medium heat. Add the onion and cook, stirring occasionally, until translucent but not browned, 3 to 4 minutes. Add the garlic and parsley and cook until the garlic is aromatic, 2 to 3 minutes.

Add the speck, lucanica, egg, and flour to the bread-milk mixture. Using your hands, thoroughly mix the ingredients until the sausage is well combined and no big pieces of bread remain. Add the onion mixture, season with salt, and mix to combine.

CONTINUED

Line a baking sheet with parchment paper. Put 140 g/1 cup flour in a shallow bowl. Divide the dough into 12 pieces and roll into balls. Working with one ball at a time, gently roll in the flour to lightly coat and put the canederli on the prepared baking sheet. Make sure that the canederli don't touch or they will stick together.

In a large pot, bring the chicken stock to a gentle simmer over medium-low heat. Season with salt. Add the canederli to the stock and simmer until tender in the center, about 10 minutes. Ladle the canederli with the stock into six individual bowls and top with grated Parmigiano-Reggiano cheese. Serve right away.

CHESTNUT-PORCINI CANEDERLI

SERVES 4 TO 6

Bruna, the chef at Cianza in Borca di Cadore, taught me this recipe. She makes it in huge batches at her restaurant, and while she sometimes adds salumi or other garnishes, this version is her favorite.

155 G/5½ OZ STALE BREAD, CUT INTO ¼-IN (6-MM) CUBES

75 G/¼ CUP + 1 TBSP WHOLE MILK, WARM, PLUS MORE AS NEEDED

40 G/1½ OZ DRIED PORCINI MUSHROOMS

2 CUPS (480 ML) BOILING WATER

1 EGG

60 G/¼ CUP WHOLE-MILK RICOTTA CHEESE, HOMEMADE (SEE PAGE 190) OR STORE-BOUGHT

55 G/2 OZ ROASTED AND PEELED CHESTNUTS, FINELY CHOPPED

KOSHER SALT

3 TBSP FINELY GRATED PARMIGIANO-REGGIANO CHEESE, PLUS MORE FOR SERVING

100 G/¾ CUP ALL-PURPOSE FLOUR, PLUS MORE FOR ROLLING

8 CUPS (2 L) CHICKEN STOCK (PAGE 189)

In a large bowl, moisten the bread with the milk and let stand for a few minutes to allow the bread to soften and absorb the milk; the bread should be fully saturated but there should be no pooling in the bottom of the bowl. If needed, add more milk, 1 Tbsp at a time.

Place the porcini in a small bowl. Pour the boiling water over the porcini and allow to soften for 10 minutes. Remove the porcini with your hands, leaving behind any dirt that has settled on the bottom of the bowl. Squeeze the porcini to remove excess water and finely chop.

Add the egg, ricotta cheese, chopped porcini, chestnuts, 1 tsp salt, and Parmigiano-Reggiano cheese to the bread mixture. Using your hands, mix the ingredients until well combined and no big pieces of bread remain.

Add the flour and gently mix until a dough is formed. Do not overmix, as this will make the canederli tough.

Line a baking sheet with parchment paper. Put 140 g/1 cup flour in a shallow bowl. Divide the dough into 12 pieces and roll into balls. Working with one ball at a time, gently roll in the flour to lightly coat and put the canederli on the prepared baking sheet. Make sure that the canederli don't touch or they will stick together.

In a large pot, bring the chicken stock to a simmer over medium-low heat. Season with salt. Add the canederli to the stock and simmer until tender in the center, about 10 minutes. Ladle the canederli and stock into individual bowls and top with grated Parmigiano-Reggiano cheese. Serve right away.

SQUASH GNOCCHI

SERVES 4

Squash gnocchi, or gnocchi di zucca, *are found in various regions, including Friuli-Venezia Giulia, Veneto, and Val d'Aosta. In Tuscany, squash gnocchi are often baked in tomato sauce, while in the north they are often served drizzled with brown butter and sage. Many people also associate* gnocchi di zucca *with Lombardy, such as around Brescia, where they are dressed with brown butter infused with garlic and rosemary.*

170 G/6 OZ RUSSET OR YUKON GOLD POTATOES

240 G/1 CUP SQUASH PURÉE (PAGE 191)

1 EGG

1 TSP KOSHER SALT

¼ TSP FRESHLY GROUND BLACK PEPPER

¼ TSP GROUND CINNAMON

85 G/½ CUP + 2 TBSP ALL-PURPOSE FLOUR, PLUS MORE FOR DUSTING

SEMOLINA FLOUR FOR DUSTING

SAUCE OF YOUR CHOICE (SUGGESTIONS FOLLOW)

In a medium pot, cover the potatoes with cold water. Bring to a simmer over medium-high heat and cook until the potatoes can be easily pierced with a skewer, 15 to 20 minutes. Drain the potatoes in a colander and set aside to cool.

When cool enough to handle, peel the potatoes and rice them into a large bowl or the bowl of a stand mixer fitted with a paddle attachment. Add the squash purée, egg, salt, pepper, and cinnamon. Mix with your hands or on medium speed until completely combined, scraping down the sides of the bowl as needed. Add the all-purpose flour and mix just until combined. Do not overmix, as this will make the gnocchi tough. The dough should be sticky and wet. This dough doesn't need to rest.

Dust 70 g/½ cup all-purpose flour on the work surface, spreading it out until it's 5 in (12 cm) in diameter. Scrape the dough from the bowl directly on top of the flour. Sprinkle the top of the dough with an additional 30 g/¼ cup all-purpose flour. This will help prevent the dough from being too sticky to roll.

Line a baking sheet with parchment paper and dust with semolina flour. Cut off a chunk of dough about the width of two fingers and cover the rest with plastic wrap. On a work surface lightly dusted with all-purpose flour, use your hands to roll the chunk into a log about ¼ in (6 mm) in diameter. Cut the log into ½-in (12-mm) pieces. Put the gnocchi on the prepared baking sheet and shape the remaining dough. Make sure that the gnocchi don't touch or they will stick together.

(To store, refrigerate on the baking sheet, covered with plastic wrap, for up to 2 days, or freeze on the baking sheet and transfer to an airtight container. Use within 1 month. Do not thaw before cooking.)

Bring a large pot filled with generously salted water to a simmer over medium-high heat. Add the gnocchi and simmer until they float to the surface, 1 to 3 minutes. Remove immediately with a slotted spoon and finish with your choice of sauce. Serve right away.

SAUCE PAIRINGS: *Traditionally, these gnocchi are paired with Tomato Sauce (page 175), Brown Butter with Sage (page 178), Fonduta (page 179), or Gorgonzola Cream Sauce (page 180).*

SAUCES

In Italy, pasta is about the noodle or dumpling, not about the sauce. The sauce is intended to complement the flavor and texture of the pasta. Every sauce should be wonderful, savory, and delicious in its own right, but it is not the primary focus of the dish. Think of the sauce as a dressing for the dumplings. The sauce should coat and cover them, but the dumplings should not be swimming in sauce.

The following recipes are a small selection of sauces that pair especially well with the dumplings in this book. I have paired many dumplings with classic sauces, based on the texture of the dumplings and how well the dumplings hold the sauce. Traditionally, many regions serve a specific dumpling only with a specific sauce, and while some modern Italian chefs are breaking from tradition, most restaurants still offer the classic pairings. Since this book is an exploration of specific regional dumplings, I am only suggesting traditional sauces to pair with each dumpling. The sauces can be used with several dumplings from different regions.

You may notice that most of the sauce recipes yield quite a bit of sauce. That's because making sauce is labor-intensive; and in most households, Nonna isn't at home all day to do the cooking. Many home cooks now prepare sauces in large batches and refrigerate or freeze them to be used later. Storing instructions are included for sauces that keep well.

SAUCE NOTES

1. Always use good stock when making a meat ragù. Don't use the thin, store-bought broth that comes in a box; make your own. The end result is immensely better. My recipe is on page 189.

2. A shout-out to my friends in Umbria. As promised, let me declare on your behalf: Umbrians finish their sauce with olive oil, never butter!

3. If your sauce is too thick, add some of the pasta cooking water or rich, warm stock, 1 Tbsp at a time, until the sauce is velvety and soft.

4. A rule of thumb about cheese: In Italy, there are many wonderful aged cheeses that are served grated on pasta. Since we cannot keep all of them in our restaurant, we think of finishing pasta this way: If a pasta is from Rome or farther south (or is served with a lamb ragù), finish it with aged Pecorino-Romano. If a pasta is from north of Rome (or is served with a meat sauce that is not lamb), finish it with Parmigiano-Reggiano. This guideline is not steadfast, of course. Italians have rules that change from home to home, village to village, and region to region. Above all, keep in mind that cheese, like sauce, is intended to enliven the dish, not overpower it. A gentle grating is all you need.

5. I like to add a small knob of butter when warming up meat ragù, as butter enriches the ragù and helps the sauce stick gently to the pasta. Individual instructions for each sauce follow the recipe.

6. When adding fresh herbs to a sauce, I always use whole herb leaves, discarding any tough stems. This prevents browning where the herbs have been cut.

PESTO

MAKES 2 CUPS (480 ML)

Basil pesto comes from Genoa, in Liguria, and is a truly beloved sauce. It can be made using different nuts and herbs, but the original is made from fresh basil, garlic, and pine nuts. Basil pesto is a rich and herbaceous sauce that, for many Americans, screams summertime. In Genoa, minestrone soup is finished with basil pesto and the sauce is also served on trofie, a regional pasta shape. Pesto is the first sauce I tasted on gnocchi, in Siena, Tuscany. It hooked me on gnocchi forever.

½ CUP (70 G) PINE NUTS
2 GARLIC CLOVES, PEELED
KOSHER SALT
4½ CUPS (130 G) FRESH BASIL LEAVES
¾ CUP (180 ML) EXTRA-VIRGIN OLIVE OIL, PLUS MORE FOR STORING AND SERVING
½ CUP (60 G) FINELY GRATED PARMIGIANO-REGGIANO CHEESE, PLUS MORE FOR SERVING
DUMPLINGS OF YOUR CHOICE, JUST COOKED

Combine the pine nuts, garlic, and 1½ tsp salt in the bowl of a food processor and pulse until finely chopped. With a rubber spatula, scrape down the sides of the bowl, then add the basil, ½ cup (120 ml) of the olive oil, and the Parmigiano-Reggiano cheese. Continue to pulse, stopping occasionally to scrape down the sides of the bowl, until the basil leaves are coarsely chopped. Turn the processor back on and add the remaining ¼ cup (60 ml) olive oil, processing until the mixture is finely chopped but not fully puréed. Turn the food processor off and scrape down the sides of the bowl several times during this process. The ingredients should be fully incorporated, with enough oil to hold the sauce together without being runny.

(To store, transfer to an airtight container and drizzle just enough oil over the top to cover—this will prevent the pesto from oxidizing and turning brown. Refrigerate for up to 4 days, or freeze for up to 1 month. To thaw, place in the refrigerator overnight or until fully thawed.)

To finish dumplings with pesto, for each serving, place a heaping 2 Tbsp of pesto in a bowl. Add the cooked dumplings along with 1 or 2 Tbsp of their cooking water and stir until coated with pesto. Season with salt, and finish with a drizzle of olive oil and grated Parmigiano-Reggiano. Serve right away.

TOMATO SAUCE

From region to region in Italy and household to household, the style and recipe for tomato-based sauces will vary. Some sauces are thick and textural, and other sauces are thin and silky. This sauce combines elements of many techniques I have learned. It is a basic sauce that pairs well with many pastas and dumplings. The addition of butter in this version was inspired by a specific recipe from Marcella Hazan—the butter softens the acid in the tomatoes and adds a lactic sweetness.

2 TBSP EXTRA-VIRGIN OLIVE OIL

4 LARGE GARLIC CLOVES, HALVED

½ LARGE YELLOW ONION, SLICED

LEAVES FROM 1 SPRIG FRESH ROSEMARY

1 BAY LEAF

½ TSP RED PEPPER FLAKES

6 CUPS (1.2 KG) CANNED WHOLE PEELED TOMATOES, PURÉED AND STRAINED

½ CUP (115 G) UNSALTED BUTTER, CUT INTO SMALL CUBES, PLUS MORE FOR SERVING

KOSHER SALT

DUMPLINGS OF YOUR CHOICE, JUST COOKED

GRATED PARMIGIANO-REGGIANO CHEESE FOR SERVING

In a medium pot, warm the olive oil over medium heat. Add the garlic, onion, rosemary, bay leaf, and red pepper flakes and cook until the onion is translucent, about 10 minutes. If the onion begins to brown, lower the heat. Add the tomatoes and butter and simmer, stirring occasionally, until the sauce is slightly thick and soft but not pasty, about 45 minutes. The butter should emulsify into the sauce. Season with salt. Set a fine-mesh strainer over a large bowl and pour the sauce into the strainer. Discard the solids in the strainer.

(To store, transfer to an airtight container and refrigerate for up to 2 days, or freeze for up to 1 month. To thaw, place in the refrigerator overnight or until fully thawed.)

To finish dumplings with sauce, for each serving, warm about ½ cup (120 ml) of the tomato sauce in a sauté pan over medium heat. Add 1½ tsp to 1 Tbsp butter per serving, depending on how naughty you feel, and gently simmer until the bubbles get large and the sauce is not watery along the edges of the pan. The sauce should be thick and silky, not dry or pasty. Add the cooked dumplings and simmer for 1 minute to let the dumplings absorb the flavor of the sauce. Spoon into serving bowls and top with grated Parmigiano-Reggiano. Serve right away.

GUANCIALE, TOMATO, AND RED ONION SAUCE

MAKES 4 CUPS (1 L)

This sauce, known as all'amatriciana, *is one of my all-time favorites. It is simple and quick to make, the ingredients are often in my refrigerator, and it is so, so delicious. If you cannot find guanciale (cured pork cheeks) at your local grocery or Italian market, pancetta or bacon makes a fine substitute. If you do not have time to make dumplings, this sauce is wonderful with many pasta shapes, but in Lazio, it is intended to be enjoyed with bucatini.*

4 OZ (115 G) GUANCIALE, CUT INTO ¼-IN (6-MM) CUBES
1 RED ONION, CUT INTO SMALL DICE
¼ TSP RED PEPPER FLAKES
4 CUPS (800 G) CANNED WHOLE PEELED TOMATOES, PURÉED AND STRAINED
KOSHER SALT AND FRESHLY GROUND BLACK PEPPER
DUMPLINGS OF YOUR CHOICE, JUST COOKED
EXTRA-VIRGIN OLIVE OIL FOR DRIZZLING
PARMIGIANO-REGGIANO CHEESE FOR GRATING

In a large sauté pan, cook the guanciale over medium heat until slightly crisp but still fatty and tender, 6 to 8 minutes. Add the onion and cook until it is soft but not browned, about 5 minutes. If the onion begins to brown, lower the heat. Add the red pepper flakes and tomatoes, turn the heat to medium-low, and simmer until the sauce is slightly reduced, 6 to 8 minutes. Season with salt and pepper.

To finish dumplings with the sauce, add six portions of cooked dumplings to the sauce along with 1 to 2 Tbsp of their cooking water. Simmer for 1 minute to let the dumplings absorb the flavor of the sauce. Drizzle with olive oil, spoon into serving bowls, and top with grated Parmigiano-Reggiano cheese. Serve right away.

BROWN BUTTER WITH SAGE

MAKES ¾ CUP (180 ML)

Butter and brown butter are used as a sauce for pasta in many regions of Italy. And in this recipe, by sauce, I mean an ample sauce—not just drizzled over pasta, but pasta generously bathed in butter! In Modena, potato gnocchi may be dressed in butter and drizzled with aged balsamic vinegar. In Rome, gnocchi alla Romana is finished with melted butter and Pecorino-Romano cheese. And, in Trento, canederli is simmered, then served with melted butter and shaved grana Trentino cheese. This brown butter sauce adds the nutty flavor of caramelized milk solids and the herbal quality of sage. It is wonderful on Traditional Spätzli (page 151), Beet Spätzli (page 153), Ricotta Gnocchetti (page 77), and Squash Gnocchi (page 168). This recipe is easily scaled up or down to make as much sauce as you need for your dumplings.

¾ CUP (170 G) UNSALTED BUTTER

12 FRESH SAGE LEAVES

KOSHER SALT

DUMPLINGS OF YOUR CHOICE, JUST COOKED

In a medium sauté pan, melt the butter with the sage over medium-low heat. Continue cooking, stirring occasionally, until the butter becomes golden brown and the milk solids separate to the bottom of the pan and turn toasty, about 10 minutes. Remove from the heat and season lightly with salt.

To finish dumplings with brown butter, add six portions of cooked dumplings to the sauce. Toss to coat and spoon into serving bowls. Serve right away.

FONDUTA

MAKES 2 CUPS (480 ML)

Fonduta is a rich, silky, elegant, and special sauce. When some of the Fontina is added to the sauce just before serving, the consistency is stringy and the sauce is called alla bava, *meaning "drool"— like drool from a dog's mouth! Fonduta is a specialty of Piedmont, a region whose history of nobility and general opulence is more than evident in the local cuisine. I first tasted fonduta in Alba at the Truffle Festival in October 2004. I walked into the festival tent and was intoxicated by the intensity of the truffle aroma. The owner of the hotel where I was staying, Nico, told me that his uncle was a chef who would be cooking at the festival. I made my way back to the kitchen and introduced myself. Next thing I knew, I was holding a bowl of pasta with fonduta and shaved truffles. Lucky, lucky me! Fonduta does not store well, so make it when you're ready to eat.*

1¾ CUPS + 2 TBSP (450 ML) HEAVY CREAM

5 OZ (140 G) FONTINA VAL D'AOSTA CHEESE

⅓ CUP (30 G) FINELY GRATED PARMIGIANO-REGGIANO CHEESE

4 EGG YOLKS

4 TBSP (55 G) UNSALTED BUTTER, AT ROOM TEMPERATURE

KOSHER SALT

FRESHLY GRATED NUTMEG

DUMPLINGS OF YOUR CHOICE, JUST COOKED

Fill a medium pot with about 2 in (5 cm) of water and bring to a simmer over medium-high heat. Make a double boiler by suspending a medium metal or heatproof glass bowl over the simmering water; be sure that the bottom of the bowl does not touch the water. Combine the cream, Fontina cheese, and Parmigiano-Reggiano cheese in the bowl and heat the mixture, whisking constantly, until smooth and thick enough to coat the back of a spoon, 5 to 7 minutes.

In a small bowl, whisk the egg yolks, then whisk in 2 to 3 Tbsp of the warm cream mixture; this will temper the yolks so that

they do not scramble when added to the cream mixture. Whisk the tempered yolks and the butter into the cream mixture and cook, whisking constantly, until the butter is incorporated and the sauce is airy, 5 to 7 minutes. Season with salt and a few swipes of nutmeg.

To finish dumplings with fonduta, portion six to eight servings of cooked dumplings into individual bowls and spoon the fonduta over the top. Serve right away.

GORGONZOLA CREAM SAUCE

MAKES 2 CUPS (480 ML)

Gorgonzola dolce is a soft, luxurious blue cheese that melts nicely. This sauce goes especially well with Winter Squash Cavatelli (page 42) and with just about any potato gnocchi.

1¾ CUPS + 2 TBSP (450 ML) HEAVY CREAM
4 OZ (110 G) GORGONZOLA DOLCE CHEESE, CUT INTO SMALL PIECES
⅓ CUP (30 G) FINELY GRATED PARMIGIANO-REGGIANO CHEESE
KOSHER SALT
FRESHLY GRATED NUTMEG
DUMPLINGS OF YOUR CHOICE, JUST COOKED
CHOPPED TOASTED WALNUTS FOR SERVING

In a medium saucepan over medium heat, combine the cream, Gorgonzola dolce cheese, and Parmigiano-Reggiano cheese and bring to a gentle simmer. Cook, whisking occasionally, until the sauce is smooth, reduced by about one-third, and thick enough to coat the back of a spoon, 7 to 10 minutes. Season with salt and a few swipes of nutmeg.

To finish dumplings with the sauce, portion four to six servings of cooked dumplings into individual bowls. Spoon the sauce over the top and sprinkle with chopped walnuts. Serve right away.

LIVER, PANCETTA, AND PORCINI RAGÙ

MAKES 2 CUPS (480 ML)

Liver adds richness and depth to this sauce. Chicken and rabbit livers have two lobes that are connected by a few veins. To clean, simply place the lobes on a cutting board and trim each side, separating the lobe from the veins. Eating liver is very common in many regions of Italy, where it is never wasted. If you think you may not like liver, give this recipe a chance—think of it as training wheels. The pancetta, porcini mushrooms, and cream balance the liver and create a wonderfully complex sauce.

2 TBSP EXTRA-VIRGIN OLIVE OIL

2½ OZ (70 G) PANCETTA, CUT INTO SMALL DICE

3 FRESH SAGE LEAVES

LEAVES FROM 1 SPRIG FRESH ROSEMARY

½ YELLOW ONION, CUT INTO SMALL DICE

5 OZ (140 G) FRESH PORCINI MUSHROOMS, SLICED

PINCH OF RED PEPPER FLAKES

8 OZ (225 G) RABBIT OR CHICKEN LIVERS, CLEANED (SEE HEADNOTE) AND FINELY CHOPPED

¼ CUP (60 ML) RED WINE

2 CUPS (480 ML) CHICKEN STOCK (PAGE 189)

½ CUP (120 ML) HEAVY CREAM

KOSHER SALT AND FRESHLY GROUND BLACK PEPPER

UNSALTED BUTTER FOR SERVING

DUMPLINGS OF YOUR CHOICE, JUST COOKED

GRATED PARMIGIANO-REGGIANO CHEESE FOR SERVING

In a large sauté pan, warm the olive oil over medium-high heat. Add the pancetta, sage, and rosemary and cook, stirring occasionally, until the pancetta is golden, 2 to 4 minutes. Add the onion, porcini, and red pepper flakes and cook until the onion is translucent, about 3 minutes. Add the livers and cook, stirring occasionally, until cooked through, about 4 minutes. Add the wine, raise the heat to high, and bring to a simmer. Simmer until the wine has evaporated, then add the stock and cream, turn the heat to medium, and simmer gently until the liquid reduces by half. Season with salt and pepper.

To finish dumplings with ragù, for each serving, warm ½ cup (120 ml) of ragù in a sauté pan over medium heat and add 1½ tsp to 1 Tbsp butter per serving, depending on how naughty you feel. Simmer gently until the bubbles get large and the sauce is not watery along the edges of the pan. Add the cooked dumplings along with 1 to 2 Tbsp of their cooking water and simmer for 1 minute to let the dumplings absorb the flavor of the sauce. Spoon into serving bowls and top with grated Parmigiano-Reggiano cheese. Serve right away.

RABBIT RAGÙ

MAKES 3 CUPS (720 ML)

Rabbit is as common in Italy as chicken is in the United States. At Lincoln, this ragù is a staple. We buy whole rabbits and use every part: the bones are made into stock, the fore- and hindquarters are used for an entrée, and the loins and bellies are ground for ragù. Often we also use the livers, heart, and kidneys when making ragù; they add great richness and flavor. If finding ground rabbit meat is challenging, check with a local farm, Italian market, or specialty butcher, and ask specifically for medium-large grind (if the rabbit is finely ground, it will cook too quickly and toughen). This sauce is well worth the effort.

3 TBSP EXTRA-VIRGIN OLIVE OIL

2 OZ (60 G) PANCETTA, PROSCIUTTO, OR BACON, FINELY CHOPPED

¼ CUP (40 G) FINELY DICED YELLOW ONION

¼ CUP (45 G) FINELY DICED FENNEL BULB

1 SPRIG FRESH ROSEMARY

3 FRESH SAGE LEAVES

2 SPRIGS FRESH THYME

2 BAY LEAVES

1 TSP RED PEPPER FLAKES

¼ CUP (50 G) CANNED WHOLE PEELED TOMATOES, PURÉED AND STRAINED

½ CUP (120 ML) RED WINE

4 CUPS (960 ML) CHICKEN STOCK (PAGE 189)

1 LB (455 G) GROUND RABBIT LOIN AND BELLY, MEDIUM-LARGE GRIND

KOSHER SALT AND FRESHLY GROUND BLACK PEPPER

UNSALTED BUTTER FOR SERVING

DUMPLINGS OF YOUR CHOICE, JUST COOKED

GRATED PARMIGIANO-REGGIANO CHEESE FOR SERVING

In a large heavy-bottomed pot, warm the olive oil over medium-high heat. Add the pancetta and cook until the fat renders and the pancetta barely begins to brown, about 4 minutes. Add the onion, fennel, rosemary, sage, thyme, bay leaves, and red pepper flakes and cook until the onion and pancetta are soft and slightly caramelized, 3 to 4 minutes. Add the tomatoes and stir to combine.

Turn the heat to low and cook until the tomato thickens and begins to caramelize, 5 to 7 minutes. Stir in the red wine, raise the heat to medium-low, and cook until the wine is almost completely evaporated, 2 to 4 minutes. Stir in the chicken stock and simmer very gently until the sauce is reduced to about one-third, about 20 minutes.

Add the rabbit to the sauce, stirring to break up any lumps, and simmer just until the meat is soft, tender, and cooked through, about 10 minutes. Rabbit is lean, so it does not require much cooking time. Season the sauce with salt and pepper and discard the herb sprigs and bay leaves.

(To store, transfer to an airtight container and refrigerate for up to 2 days, or freeze for up to 1 month. To thaw, place in the refrigerator overnight or until fully thawed.)

To finish dumplings with the ragù, for each serving, warm ½ cup (120 ml) of ragù in a sauté pan over medium heat and add 1½ tsp to 1 Tbsp butter per serving, depending on how naughty you feel. Gently simmer about 4 minutes, until the bubbles get large and the sauce is not watery along the edges of the pan. Add the cooked dumplings and simmer for 1 minute to let the dumplings absorb the flavor of the sauce. Spoon into serving bowls and top with grated Parmigiano-Reggiano cheese. Serve right away.

LAMB RAGÙ

MAKES 4 CUPS (960 ML)

Lamb (young sheep) is a staple protein in many regions of Italy. A specialty in Rome is pajata, *baby lamb intestine cooked in tomato sauce. In Abruzzo, mutton (adult sheep) is stewed and served as a main dish, or as a sauce on pasta. The lamb in this ragù is braised as chunks rather than ground. Depending on the size of your dumplings, you can shred or chop the meat after it is braised, then add it back into the sauce. As a rule of thumb, the meat in a ragù is a garnish, so make sure that the meat is always smaller than the dumpling or pasta size.*

1½ LB (680 G) LAMB SHOULDER, TRIMMED OF EXCESS FAT AND CUT INTO 1-IN (2.5-CM) CUBES

KOSHER SALT AND FRESHLY GROUND BLACK PEPPER

3 TBSP EXTRA-VIRGIN OLIVE OIL

½ MEDIUM YELLOW ONION, CUT INTO MEDIUM DICE

2 BAY LEAVES

1 SPRIG FRESH ROSEMARY

2 TBSP TOMATO PASTE

½ CUP (120 ML) DRY RED WINE

2 CUPS (480 ML) LAMB STOCK OR CHICKEN STOCK (PAGE 189)

UNSALTED BUTTER FOR SERVING

DUMPLINGS OF YOUR CHOICE, JUST COOKED

GRATED AGED PECORINO CHEESE FOR SERVING

Preheat the oven to 300°F (150°C).

Season the lamb cubes with salt and pepper. In a large sauté pan, warm the olive oil over high heat. Working in batches, add the lamb cubes in a single layer, being careful not to overcrowd the pan. Sear until golden brown, turning to brown all sides, 6 to 8 minutes. Transfer to a roasting pan, leaving enough oil in the sauté pan to coat the bottom.

Set the sauté pan over medium heat. Add the onion, bay leaves, and rosemary and sauté until the onion is translucent and soft, about 5 minutes. Add the tomato paste and cook until the tomato caramelizes (it will begin to stick to the bottom of the pan and turn dark red), 4 to 6 minutes. Add the wine and stir to scrape up any flavorful brown bits from the bottom of the pan. Raise the heat to medium-high and cook until the wine has almost completely evaporated, 3 to 4 minutes. Add the lamb stock and bring to a simmer. Season lightly with salt and pepper, being careful not to overseason, as the flavors will concentrate during the braising process. Once the stock mixture is simmering, add it to the lamb in the roasting pan.

Tightly cover the roasting pan with a lid or aluminum foil and braise in the oven until the lamb is tender and easily pulled apart, about 1 hour. (Braise for more time as needed, checking every 5 minutes.) Remove from the oven, uncover, and let the lamb cool to room temperature in the braising liquid. When cool enough to handle, shred the meat with two forks, or remove it from the sauce, coarsely chop, and return to the sauce. Discard the rosemary sprig and bay leaves.

(To store, transfer to an airtight container and refrigerate for up to 2 days, or freeze for up to 1 month. To thaw, place in the refrigerator overnight or until fully thawed.)

To finish dumplings with the ragù, for each serving, warm ½ cup (120 ml) of ragù in a sauté pan over medium heat and add 1½ tsp to 1 Tbsp butter per serving, depending on how naughty you feel. Gently simmer for about 4 minutes, until the bubbles get large and the sauce is not watery along the edges of the pan. Add the cooked dumplings along with 1 to 2 Tbsp of their cooking water and simmer for 1 minute to let the dumplings absorb the flavor of the sauce. Spoon into serving bowls and top with grated pecorino cheese. Serve right away.

BEEF RAGÙ

MAKES 6 CUPS (1.4 L)

This hearty sauce is deeply savory and intense. The richness and complexity of the slowly cooked beef brisket and tomato paste complement the rustic dumplings and showcase the true craft that goes into Italian home cooking. Ground lamb shoulder or beef chuck can be substituted for the brisket— just check the meat as it cooks, because different cuts will cook at different rates. When the meat is finished cooking, it will be completely separated from the fat and full of rich, concentrated flavor.

½ CUP (120 ML) EXTRA-VIRGIN OLIVE OIL

3 OZ (85 G) PANCETTA OR PROSCIUTTO, FINELY CHOPPED

2¼ LB (1 KG) GROUND BEEF BRISKET

1 YELLOW ONION, CUT INTO MEDIUM DICE

2 GARLIC CLOVES, THINLY SLICED

2 BAY LEAVES

½ TSP RED PEPPER FLAKES

½ CUP (140 G) TOMATO PASTE

¾ CUP (180 ML) RED WINE

2½ QT (2.7 L) CHICKEN STOCK (PAGE 189), PLUS MORE AS NEEDED

KOSHER SALT AND FRESHLY GROUND BLACK PEPPER

UNSALTED BUTTER FOR SERVING

DUMPLINGS OF YOUR CHOICE, JUST COOKED

GRATED PARMIGIANO-REGGIANO CHEESE FOR SERVING

In a large pot, warm the olive oil over medium heat. Add the pancetta and beef brisket and cook, stirring occasionally, until the meat is cooked and browned bits stick to the bottom of the pot, 8 to 10 minutes. If the drippings on the bottom of the pot become too dark or look like they will burn, lower the heat.

With a slotted spoon, transfer the meat to a bowl, leaving about 3 Tbsp fat in the pot and discarding any excess. Add the onion, garlic, bay leaves, and red pepper flakes and sauté over medium heat until the onion is translucent but not brown, about 4 minutes. The moisture from the onion will help deglaze the pan (dislodge the browned bits).

Add the tomato paste and cook until the tomato caramelizes (it will begin to stick to the bottom of the pan and turn dark red), 4 to 6 minutes. If the tomato paste gets too dark, lower the heat. Add the wine, raise the heat to medium-high, and bring to a simmer. Use a wooden spoon to scrape up the browned bits from the bottom of the pot and simmer until the wine has almost completely evaporated, 5 to 7 minutes.

Add the chicken stock and bring to a gentle simmer. Return the meat to the pot, turn the heat to medium-low, and simmer gently—the liquid should bubble lazily—until the meat has become tender and the sauce has gradually reduced and become rich. Be patient; this will take about 3 hours. Be careful not to let the sauce boil. If the sauce becomes too thick, add up to ½ cup (120 ml) additional chicken stock. Season lightly with salt and pepper and discard the bay leaves.

(To store, transfer to an airtight container and refrigerate for up to 2 days, or freeze for up to 1 month. To thaw, place in the refrigerator overnight or until fully thawed.)

To finish dumplings with the ragù, for each serving, warm about ½ cup (120 ml) of ragù in a sauté pan over medium heat and add 1½ tsp to 1 Tbsp butter per serving, depending on how naughty you feel. Gently simmer about 4 minutes, until the bubbles get large and the sauce is not watery along the edges of the pan. Add the cooked dumplings and simmer for 1 minute to let the dumplings absorb the flavor of the sauce. Top with grated Parmigiano-Reggiano cheese and season with salt and pepper. Serve right away.

LARDER

The following few recipes are staples that are best made at home, rather than purchasing at the store. Especially when it is hard to find artisan-quality and specialty ingredients, mastering basic techniques at home will not just provide the magical "*I made that!*" delight, but also will make the end result of your dumplings and sauces fabulous. These few pantry items can be used when cooking many dishes, not just the recipes in this book. After practicing once or twice, you will realize how simple each technique really is.

CHICKEN STOCK

MAKES 1¾ QT (1.7 L)

I refer to homemade chicken stock as liquid gold, because it is. When I roast chickens at home, I freeze the leftover carcasses in a resealable plastic bag and, when I have several, I make a big batch of stock. I like to make a second, richer, stock by repeating the process: after I simmer the roasted bones and water, I strain the stock, and then use it instead of water, along with newly roasted bones, to make a secondary stock. This secondary stock will be especially rich and gelatinous. Whether primary or secondary stock, the gelatinous texture is paramount in making a rich ragù or soup. You can certainly use this technique with pork, beef, or lamb (see Lamb Stock, below). Simply substitute the bones of your choice and proceed with the same technique; beef and lamb, which are richer meats, will require at least 8 hours of simmering.

The fat (a.k.a. schmaltz) that is skimmed off the stock after chilling is delicious spread onto baguette slices, then topped with prosciutto and sea salt. If you have a generous amount of schmaltz, add a few Parmigiano-Reggiano rinds and simmer for about 1 hour; the cheese-flavored fat can be used for sautéing vegetables.

5 LB (2.3 KG) CHICKEN BONES

Preheat the oven to 450°F (230°C). Line a baking sheet with parchment paper and lay the chicken bones on top. Do not overlap the bones. Roast the bones until nicely browned, about 20 minutes.

Transfer the roasted bones to a 6-qt (5.7-L) stockpot and fill with just enough cold water to cover the bones. Bring the water to a rapid simmer over high heat, then immediately lower the heat to medium to achieve a gentle, lazy simmer. Simmer for 6 to 8 hours. If the stock simmers too briskly, the fat will emulsify into the stock, rendering the stock greasy. If the stock reduces too quickly, add a bit of additional water. This should not be necessary, and ideally the stock will reduce by one-third to one-half when cooking slowly. As the stock is simmering, use a spoon or ladle to skim off and discard any foamy, dark impurities that rise to the top.

Set a fine-mesh sieve over a large, heavy-duty plastic container. Pour the stock through the sieve into the container and discard the chicken bones and any debris. Transfer the stock to airtight containers and refrigerate until cool. When the stock is cold, remove the fat by gently scooping it from the top with a spoon.

To store the chicken fat, transfer it to an airtight container and refrigerate for up to 1 month. To store the stock, refrigerate for up to 1 week, or freeze for up to 2 months.

LAMB STOCK: *Use 5 lb (2.3 kg) lamb bones instead of chicken bones, roasting and then simmering them for 8 hours as directed in the recipe.*

HOMEMADE RICOTTA

MAKES 2 LB (900 G)

Homemade ricotta is splendid. Making fresh cheese is much easier than you might think, and the end result is creamier and richer than most store-bought ricottas. This recipe is made with mostly whole milk and buttermilk, but contains some half-and-half, too. The end result is rich in texture and flavor, but not overwhelmingly rich like a cream-based cheese. The by-product, whey, is wonderful—don't throw it away! It will keep for about 1 week, refrigerated, and is great in dishes when you want a lactic and acidic flavor. My favorite uses include whey-braised pork (instead of milk-braised) and wilting spinach with whey and preserved lemon.

5 QT (4.7 L) WHOLE MILK

5 CUPS (1.2 L) BUTTERMILK

3 CUPS (720 ML) HALF-AND-HALF

Combine the milk, buttermilk, and half-and-half in a large, heavy-bottomed pot and cook over high heat, stirring gently every few minutes to distribute the heat evenly, for 6 to 8 minutes. When curds start to form, stop stirring. Bring the mixture to 175°F (80°C), as measured on an instant-read thermometer, then turn off the heat and let cool, without disturbing, until the mixture is almost at room temperature. Carefully transfer the pot to the refrigerator and let cool completely.

Meanwhile, line a large fine-mesh strainer with a double layer of cheesecloth and set the strainer over a large, deep bowl so that the whey can drain. When fully cooled, remove the pot from the refrigerator and gently ladle the curds into the strainer. Cover with plastic wrap, refrigerate, and let drain overnight.

The following day, transfer the ricotta to airtight containers. Seal tightly and refrigerate for up to 1 week. Do not freeze ricotta.

SQUASH PURÉE

MAKES 6 CUPS (1.4 KG)

This basic recipe can be used to make many dishes—thin the purée with rich chicken stock and serve it as a soup, layer it between lasagna noodles and ricotta cheese for a hearty baked pasta dish, or use it as a base for squash pie. When using this purée to make dumplings, it is best to use freshly made, warm purée. As the squash purée cools, moisture escapes (by evaporation) and the purée loses its smooth texture.

2 MEDIUM BUTTERNUT SQUASH, PEELED, SEEDED, AND CUT INTO 1-IN (2.5-CM) CUBES
2 TBSP EXTRA-VIRGIN OLIVE OIL

Preheat the oven to 350°F (180°C). Place the squash in a large shallow baking dish. Drizzle with the olive oil and toss to coat. Cover the squash with parchment paper, then cover the baking dish with aluminum foil. Bake until tender, 25 to 35 minutes.

Using a ricer, food mill, or fine-mesh sieve, purée the squash until smooth. Use immediately, or store in airtight containers in the refrigerator for up to 5 days. Do not freeze squash purée.

GLOSSARY

This informal glossary explains the background and regional variations of some of the dumplings included in this book that are lesser known outside of Italy.

CANEDERLI

Canederli, also referred to as *knödel*, *gnocchi di pane*, and *canedeli*, are considered *cucina povera*, or "cuisine of the poor." These dumplings provide a filling dish that can use stale bread garnished with bits and pieces of more costly ingredients. The dumplings are primarily made from bread, eggs, and flour; cheese, meat, herbs, and vegetables can be added. Traditionally, at higher elevations, vegetables were not in abundance; at lower elevations with milder climates, greens grow more abundantly and are added to the dumpling. Just like all regional dumplings, some recipe variations—in this case, of regional cheeses, meats (speck, liver, brains), or fruit—occur from village to village.

CAVATELLI

Cavatelli is commonly found in Campania, Puglia, Sicily, Calabria, and Basilicata. These little dumplings go by many different names and have regional significance based on the types of flour used and the regional dialect. Consider *cavatelli* a generic name for the shape of dumpling made by rolling a small piece of tender dough over a grooved surface like a board, called a *cavarola* in Basilicata, or a *crivu*, a specific basket, in Calabria. Other names include *orecchie di prete* ("priest's ears"; similar to orecchiette) in Basilicata, *cavateddri* in Calabria, and *cavatello* in Puglia. All have an elongated shape that is hollowed and rolled, although length can vary.

CHICCHE DELLA NONNA

Chicche della nonna translates as "grandmother's gnocchi" (or *del nonno* for "grandfather"). Recipes often combine potato, ricotta, and eggs, making the dumplings soft and tender. Chicche are easy to make and are delicious with creamy tomato sauce or simply with melted butter and grated Parmigiano-Reggiano. These dumplings are rustic and comforting to eat, and are a typical dish that a grandmother would make for her grandchildren.

FRASCARELLI

There are versions of frascarelli, under different names, from Lazio, Trentino, Tuscany, Marche, and Puglia. Frascarelli, made simply by moistening flour with water and sifting out the resulting clumps, can be served as pasta with a sauce or as a dumpling simmered in broth. In each region, the ingredients may be altered. In Trentino, they are called *milchfrigelen*, and buckwheat flour is substituted, while in Marche or Puglia, eggs may be added to the water before moistening the flour. In Lazio, frascarelli may be added to a brothy soup, similar to the dumpling soup Pisarei e Faso (page 105), with pancetta, celery, bay leaf, and tomato.

GNOCCHI RICCI

Gnocchi ricci means "curly gnocchi," and it refers to the curled-up sides of the dumpling. It is from the Lazio region, specifically the province of Rieti or, even more specifically, the town of Amatrice, north of Rome. This was the typical dish served on feast days, or on Sundays to noble families, but it is not widely known among the people in nearby villages. The tradition of this dumpling was almost forgotten, until the town revived it at a public workshop in 2004. Since then, the village has dedicated a spring festival to gnocchi ricci. The texture is delightfully regional: rustic, hearty, and very soulful.

There are two ways to make gnocchi ricci. The most traditional is to join two doughs together, while the other is to mix all the ingredients together like traditional pasta dough. Sometimes strained pasta sauce is used instead of some of the water in the dough. I have included both recipes, and both are equally delicious.

GNUDI

Gnudi are dumplings made with ricotta. Some people deem gnudi to be gnocchi made from ricotta; others consider them to be something different altogether. I consider gnudi to be a dumpling, in the gnocchi family, that's made from ricotta.

Gnudi, meaning "naked," are thought to be naked because they are without the pasta that surrounds the filling of a stuffed pasta such as ravioli.

MALFATTI

Malfatti, dumplings made from finely chopped cooked greens and ricotta cheese or eggs, are very similar to gnudi (see Gnudi, at left) and can be considered part of the gnudi family.

Malfatti are proof that Italians have a great sense of humor, even when it comes to naming dumplings. *Malfatti* translates as "poorly shaped" or "badly formed," but the dumplings are absolutely lovely. When made into small versions, they are called *malfatini* ("tiny malfatti"). Malfatti can be served with a sauce or placed in a dish and baked in the oven (*al forno*) and topped with grated cheese.

SPÄTZLI

Spätzli, a rustic dumpling commonly associated with Austria or Germany, is quite prevalent in the Dolomites and mountainous northern regions of Italy. This is one dumpling that is truly regional in Italy—it is rarely seen in the south of the country. Spätzli is a simple recipe, consisting of eggs, flour, salt, and milk or water, sometimes with the addition of spinach, beets, or an alternative grain like buckwheat, whole wheat, or farro.

Centuries ago, this dumpling was shaped by hand or with a spoon, by scraping bits of dough off a wooden cutting board directly into boiling water. The shape resembled small birds, giving rise to the name *spätzli*, which translates to "little sparrow" in German. Since then, several devices have been invented to form the dough, and there are many ways of extruding this dumpling. If you don't have a spätzli maker, you can use a colander or the large holes of a flat grater and push the dough through the holes with a spatula.

STRANGOLAPRETI

Bread-based dumplings such as strangolapreti and canederli (see Canederli, page 192) can be found in several regions of Italy; they are traditionally from alpine regions. In very remote villages, where winter weather causes isolation due to severe cold and mountainous terrain, bread was baked or acquired weekly, or even monthly. The use of stale bread was an economical way to utilize a pantry item like old bread and stretch other, more expensive or seasonally limited ingredients, such as vegetables, cured meat, and cheese. Bread crumb–based gnocchi are typically served as an appetizer, drizzled with melted butter, or served in broth.

Strangolapreti is a traditional dish of Trentino and the northern Italian mountainous regions. It is a variation of the Tuscan *strozzapreti*, translated as "priest stranglers," which are made with ricotta and greens rather than the bread-crumb base of the north.

Lore about priest stranglers can be heard in Friuli, Marche, Lazio, Abruzzo, Calabria, and Sicily. There are many versions of the story behind strangolapreti: Some tell of a gluttonous priest who ate too fast and choked. Others warn that the priests have too delicate of a palate to swallow such a rustic, hearty gnocchi. Still others say that this dish is so delicious it is perfect for feeding a priest.

TROFIE

Trofie, also known as Ligurian dumplings, were originally made with bread crumbs and potato in the dough. More recently, the standard dough has been made with flour and water, sometimes with the addition of chestnut flour or potato and egg. Trofie are known for their long, twisted shape, which is achieved by rolling small pieces of dough to make a short rope, then reversing and pulling the dough at an angle. I first tasted this pasta in Sestri Levante, south of Genoa, slathered with pesto. It was one of the most memorable meals I have ever eaten.

INDEX

RECCHIETTE. GNOCCHI RICCI.
SAFFRON AND POTATO GNOCCHI
RICOTTA GNOCHETTI. CAZZELLIT
ROYALE BOLOGNESE. DONDERET
GNOCCHI ALLA BAVA. FRASCARE
UGELI. CHICKPEA GNOCCHETTI
BUCKWHEAT AND RICOTTA GNOC
GNOCCHI ALL'ORTICA. DUNDER
PISAREI E FASO. RICOTTA CAVAT
EMOLINA TROFIE. PASSATELLI.
STROZZAPRETI. RUSTIC MALFAT
CHICCHE DELLA NONNA. PINCI.
CICIONES. CECAMARITI. DONZEL
ASTA GRATTUGIATA. SORCETTI